Exhibition Design

GLOUCESTER MASSACHUSETTS

ROCKPORT PUBLISHERS

Copyright © 2006 by LOFT Publications

First published in the United States of America by
Rockport Publishers, a member of
Quayside Publishing Group
33 Commercial Street
Gloucester, MA 01930-0589
Telephone: (978) 282-9590
Fax: (978) 283-2742
www.rockpub.com

ISBN: 1-59253-280-2

Texts: Llorenç Bonet

Editor Assistant: Martin Rolshoven

Art Director: Mireia Casanovas Soley

Graphic Design and Layout: Ignasi Gracia

Editorial project:
2006 © **LOFT** Publications
Via Laietana 32, 4.º of. 92
08003 Barcelona, Spain
Tel.: +34 932 688 088
Fax: +34 932 687 073
loft@loftpublications.com
www.loftpublications.com

Printed in Spain

"The time I spent working in Barcelona was a **shining**

Mies van der Rohe
Letter to *Arquitectura* magazine, Madrid, 1957

moment in my life."

Introduction

Ephemeral architecture, conceived to accommodate temporary events, has served as a testing ground throughout the twentieth century. The most vanguard innovations and ideas, as of yet untried, have appeared in international events; this historical line can be seen as much in the art exhibition pavilion of J.M. Olbrich in Damstadt, 1901, as it can in MVRDV's Dutch pavilion in the Hannover trade fair, 2000.

During their short-lived existences, these installations are visited by a large number of people, allowing the architect to evaluate how well the proposal functions and whether or not it is accepted by the general public. Their temporary quality also means that they can be easily forgotten if unsuccessful.

Today, this type of construction has become a model to follow when it comes to projecting permanent buildings: solutions, which adapt to a low budget, a quick construction process, and even the need to be transportable, have been used by many architects in the conception of perennial buildings. The Tomihiro Museum is a good example, since the simplicity of the assembly process draws on an ephemeral construction.

Despite the fact that today's triumphant architecture is spectacular, solid, and monumental, innovation and vanguard ideas continue to be a focus of investigation, as shown by architects like Cirugeda, Exyzt, or The Next Enterprise. The innovative spirit apparent in Bruno Taut's Glass Pavilion (Cologne, 1914), Mies Van der Rohe's German Pavilion (Barcelona, 1929), Alvar Aalto's Finnish Pavilion (Venice, 1957), and Bukminster Fuller's American Pavilion (Montreal, 1967) lives on in these architects. They all share the experience of taking on ephemeral architecture as unexplored territory; and while they have done so with diverse perspectives, it has always been with the same pioneering spirit.

The architecture developed for international trade fairs, although given little recognition, is some of the most complicated: the pavilions and stands need to be designed and assembled in a very short time period, and they must house complex programs within a small area. A stand has to fulfill the role of exhibitor, since it must present the product, but it must also be a pleasant space that inspires confidence, and where the customer feels comfortable. Furthermore, it should be clear that the company responsible for the financing is in control. Architects, therefore, are confronted with a difficult challenge, to which they must apply the most varied solutions, materials and typologies, and of course, the field's heritage.

Pavilion O$_2$

Architect: Klaus Schmidhuber

Address:
Schmidhuber and Partner
Nederlinger Strasse 21, 80638 Munich, Germany
+49 89 157 997
www.schmidhuber.de
info@schmidhuber.de

Fair: CeBIT 2005, Hannover, Germany
Other cities: No
Primary material: Plastic
Photos: © Wolfgang Oberle

This company pavilion had to house different spaces, such as areas for computers, meeting rooms, and a bar. The architects decided on a diaphanous space where the different uses would be separated by small platforms set at different heights. This way very different spaces could be created without the need for walls. The staggered layout of the spaces allowed the integration of the VIP room with the rest of the space, although it was situated on the second floor, where it was possible to view the entire pavilion while maintaining its intimacy.

The ceiling is the feature that unifies the project and also acts as an advertising board. The methacrylate rods are reminiscent of the sea's rolling waves or a large moving cloud of gas, combined with the name of the brand, that can be interpreted as a chemical formula, represented as a molecule composed of two oxygen atoms. On the blue surface created by the rods, it is also possible to write slogans, thanks to the points of light incorporated in each rod.

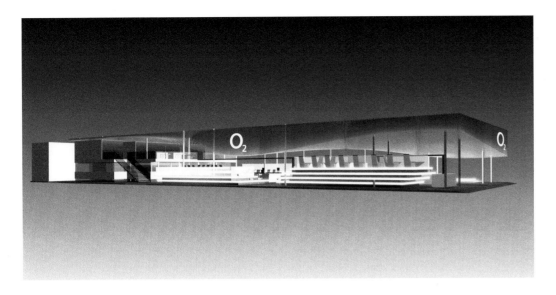

General view

The undulating lines on the ceiling are reminiscent of the waves of the sea, which, apart from making this space unique within the fair, generated a sensation of well-being and comfort.

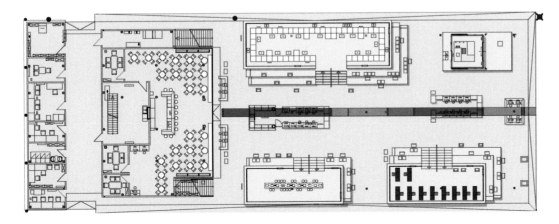

Plan

The second floor overlooks the entire stand, and offers a much closer view of the ceiling, satisfying those clients who wanted to know how the pavilion was designed.

Platforms raised above the floor of the stand allowed the designers to segragate spaces with different functions, without the need for internal partitions.

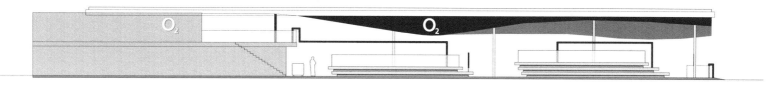

Side elevation

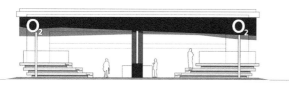

Front elevation

Saloni

Architect: Francesc Rifé

Address:
    Rife Design
    Escoles Pies 25, 08017 Barcelona, Spain
        +34 934 141 288
www.rife-design.com
f@rife-design.com

Fair: Cevisama, Valencia, Spain
Other cities: No
Primary material: Serigraphied glass
Photos: © Eugeni Pons

The Saloni stand in the Cevisama trade fair in Valencia 2005 had to include a complex program of display stands, offices, meeting rooms, and a large bar restaurant, including a kitchen. It also needed various entrances, as the designers predicted a daily influx of merchandise as well as a large number of visitors from the public.

To satisfy all the requirements, the architects divided the stand into small pavilions and separated all the functions. This created an open space, following the Mediterranean courtyard typology, which functioned as distributor and as a multi-purpose area, depending on the need. The designers created a unified stand by using the same materials in all the pavilions and glass partitions that repeatedly show one of the company's first ceramic designs. The translucent quality of these panels lends the space enough visual permeability to maintain the spatial union, but without taking any of the privacy away from the pavilions.

Apart from this lattice-based solution, the bigger pavilions were mounted on a platform with built-in lights, creating the impression that the volumes were suspended. The circular bench, lit from below in the middle of the courtyard, formed part of this light show. This indirect lighting gave the stand a warm, pleasant atmosphere.

The large glass front with screen-printing of the brand's name served both as publicity and to create a transitional zone to the inside of the pavilion.

Rendering

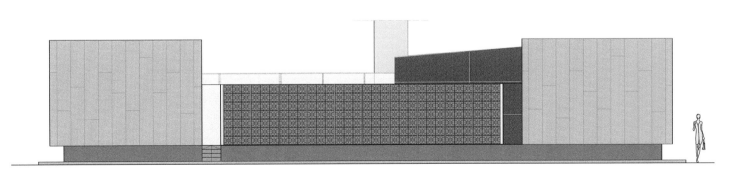

Elevation

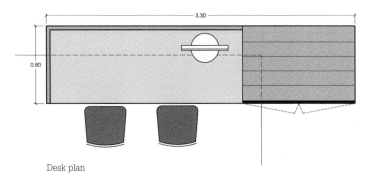

Desk plan

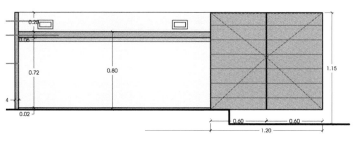

Interior elevation

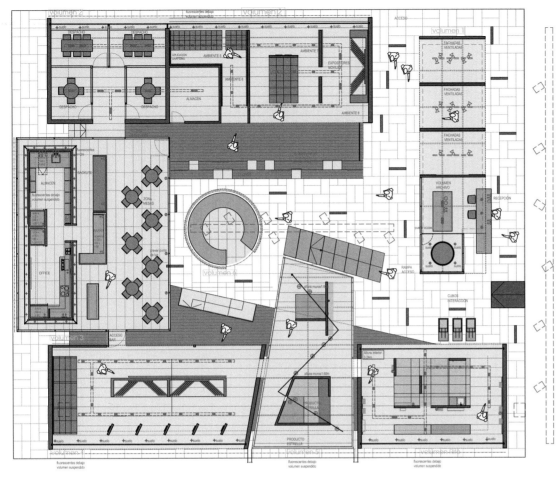

Plan

By creating small pavilions around a central courtyard, the architects designed a different interior for each use while at the same time maintaining uniformity from the outside.

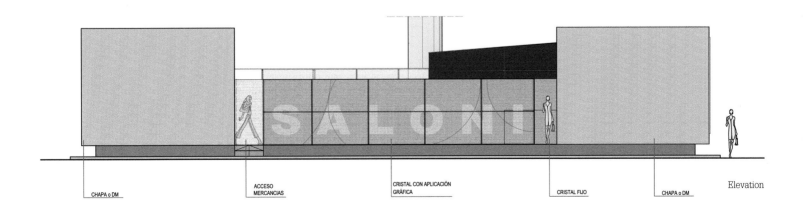

CHAPA o DM

ACCESO MERCANCIAS

CRISTAL CON APLICACIÓN GRÁFICA

CRISTAL FIJO

CHAPA o DM

Elevation

The traditional patterns on the glass created a translucent background in the central courtyard, while also giving privacy to the meeting room.

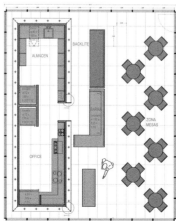

Back light bar plan

Rendering

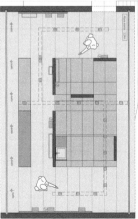

Plan

The purity of the lines in the display stands maintained the feeling of serenity and elegance throughout the set-up.

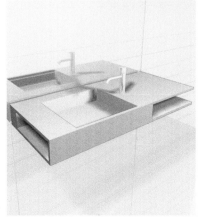

Corian washbasin

Nobel Peace Center

Architect: David Adjaye

Address:
   Adjaye and Associates
   23-28 Penn Street, N1 5DL London, United Kingdom
      +44 20 7739 4969
www.adjaye.com
info@adjaye.com

Location: City Hall Square, Oslo, Norway
Other Cities: No
Primary material: Concrete
Photos: © Timothy Soar

In 2000 the Norwegian parliament approved the construction of a permanent peace museum, and chose a proposal from a competition won by David Adjaye. Adjaye is recognized among British architects for his international projection, and known for his spatial combinations, elegant use of color, and inclusion of surprising but pleasing shapes.

The new museum was built in an old railway station dating back to 1875. Adjaye worked with artists Chris Ofili (Turner prize winner), who helped with the projection of the cafeteria, and David Small, who collaborated in the design of the audiovisual projection spaces. However, the most innovative feature is the large pergola that presides over the entrance to the building, which acts as a transitional space between the city and the museum. It consists of a parallelepiped open on two sides and made from concrete; the entire surface is riddled with small holes that trace the outline of a world map in an attempt to announce the museum's international projection. The convex domed floor and ceiling modifies the viewer's perception and serve as the main feature of this work.

Adjaye works with spatial sensations, which he calls "spatial manipulation": with very few objects he manages to imprint visitors with sensations from the building. Despite being made of concrete, the pergola appears to be very light, thanks to the large surface area and its fine profile. This gives an architecturally ephemeral image, although in fact it is a solid element that imparts order to the museum's façade.

The holes in the pavilion trace the outline of the five continents, a symbol of the museum's global outlook.

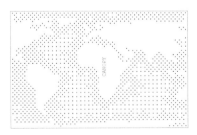

Pergola plan

The pavilion, with its slightly convex roof and floor, creates an interesting transition point between the building and the surrounding urban landscape.

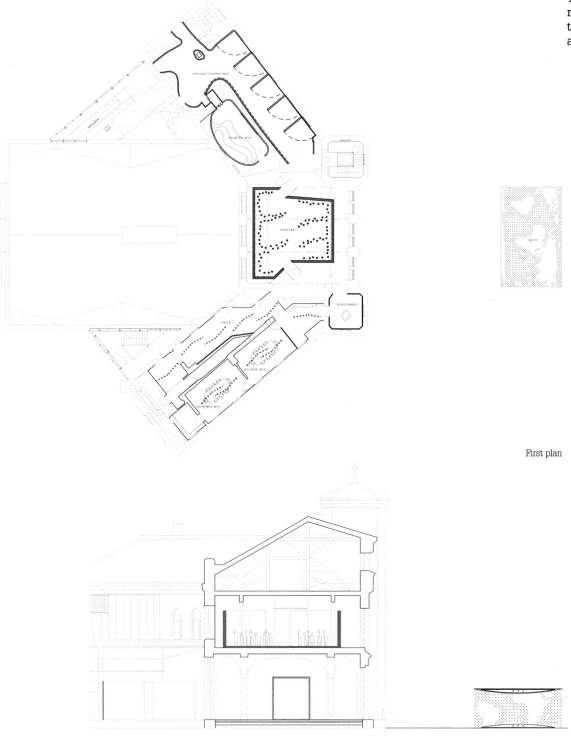

First plan

Partial section

The building's renovation maintained several old features, such as the iron columns and coffered ceilings, but at the same time completely updated the interior.

Innoval

Architect: Toni Arola

Address:
    Estudio Arola
    Lope de Vega 106, 3.º, 08005 Barcelona, Spain
        +34 933 075 369
estudioarola@hotmail.com

Fair: Alimentaria 2005, Barcelona, Spain
Other cities: No
Primary material: Orange color plates
Photos: © Eugeni Pons

Toni Arola's studio was commissioned to design the scenery of the stand to accommodate the food fair's Innoval 2004, an award given to innovative designs in the food sector. It was also responsible for the design, in the same space, of the Triptólemos foundation display stand, which explained the importance of advances in the food world throughout history.

The strategy for differentiating the two programs consisted of giving the historical display a museum-style setting, while applying a much freer scenery to show the Innoval products. The first part of the stand was set up with rectangular panels, which alternated objects in display cases with text about the exhibition. Black was the dominant color, so the area worked as an antechamber to the theatrical setting of the second area, which imitated the layout of a great banquet. Objects from the competition were laid out on large tables with white tablecloths and arranged around a large mobile made from yellow plates. This mobile, hanging from the ceiling, acted as a visual lure, but since it could be seen from the entrance to the pavilion, it was not possible to tell what it was composed of. The illumination from the colors altered the intensity of the light, giving it the appearance of a large lamp, and only on closer examination could the plates be seen hanging in the air as if someone had thrown them from the banquet tables.

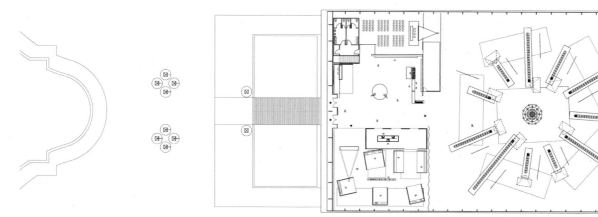

The yellow plates hanging from the center of the pavilion created a constantly changing light effect, which was visible from the entrance.

Plan

Renders

The layout of the display stands as banquet tables, organized around a mobile of suspended plates, helped lend order to a disorderly space.

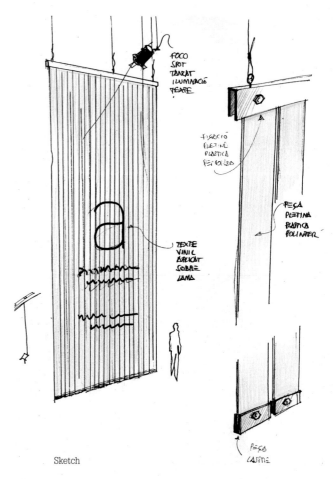

Sketch

ENVASADO CANNING & BOTTLING EN

CALOR HEAT

Sketch

Toyota

Architect: Jordi Hernández, Juan Roberto Vázquez

Address:
   Indissoluble
   Passatge de la Pau 11, 08002 Barcelona, Spain
         +34 934 121 075
www.indissoluble.com
info@indissoluble.com

Fair: Forum 2004, Barcelona, Spain
Other cities: No
Primary material: Serigraphied glass
Photos: © David Cardelús

At Barcelona's Forum 2004 Toyota presented its prototypes of ecological vehicles, one of the company's most recent fields of research.

The pavilion had to be installed beneath the Forum's massive photovoltaic panel, a privileged location since it was one of the venue's thoroughfares and it dominated one side of the venue. However, two obstacles had to be overcome: the strong winds coming from the coast, which determined the construction, and the fact that the visual impact of the photovoltaic panel overshadowed any nearby construction.

The architects consequently worked with the colors of the floor to delineate the pavilion's space: the wood from the circulation areas and the stained concrete stood out from the gray panel and were easily visible from a distance. A sixteen-foot high structure was also set up, supported by the structure of the panel, which stood out over the project and acted as the stand's identifier. This structure continued beneath the panel, directing the public towards the three bodies of the pavilion, thereby creating continuity between the inside and the outside and softening the heavy concrete walls.

In order to establish coherence within the exhibition in the least intrusive manner, the architects purposely left the materials unpolished and selected simple features.

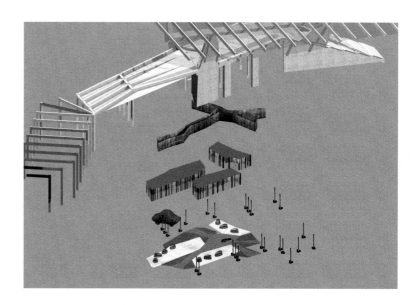

Rendering

Rendering

The bench outside with the silhouette of Toyota's new ecological line created a visual antecedent to the pavilion, which is hidden beneath the photovoltaic panel.

The elevated structure generated a directional axis, thereby creating continuity between the exterior features and the interior pavilions.

Canopy

Architects: Eric Bunge, Mimi Honag

Address:
   Narchitects
   147 Essex Street, New York, NY 10002, USA
        +1 2 122 532 853
www.narchitects.com
n@narchitects.com

Location: PS1 Art Centre
Other Cities: No
Primary material: Bamboo
Photos: © Narchitects

Canopy is a temporary structure built in the central courtyard of the PS1 Art Centre as part of its summer activities program. It is designed to give space for concerts in the evenings and activities during the day.

The architects wanted to experiment with bamboo as a construction material and use it to create the metaphor of a dense woodland landscape. Arches of bamboo cover most of the space, like vaults, leaving some clearings, which regulate the humidity and temperature. This layout allows for four different rooms. In the biggest room a shallow pool was constructed to give off humidity. Sprinklers were installed in another room to create a more humid zone, although not as humid as the third room, which is a living bamboo forest with constant rainfall. The fourth room is drier, with sand. By designing these four different areas, the rooms could be used, despite the intense heat that New York suffers in summer, for the daytime activities, often attended by families with children, as well as evening parties.

Before work began, the designers calculated the maximum curvature that the bamboo could support, as well as the amount of humidity needed to manipulate it. This way, the architects and the group of final-year students that collaborated in the construction were able to control the material and to predict how the color would change from the malleable green of the first few days to brown at the end of the installation period, when the arches could no longer be moved.

The bamboo arches totally transformed PS1's arid courtyard, making it one of the most popular meeting points among New Yorkers.

landscape   weather

CANOPY

A canopy built with freshly cut green bamboo turns from green to tan over the summer

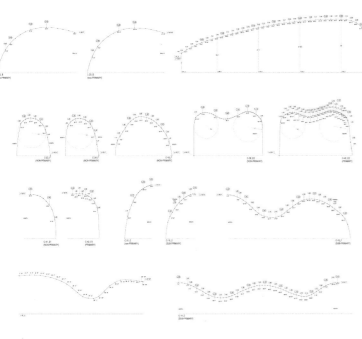

Arc profiles

Dips in the canopy provoke different modes of lounging in four distinct environments.

Sand Hump	Pool Pad	Fog Pad	Rainforest
100 deg 5% humidity	90 deg 15% humidity	80 deg 90% humidity	70 deg 100% humidity

Pinches in the canopy produce a range of shadow densities.

July 21st: 11:00...   ... 2:00   ... 6:00

Concept diagrams

The juxtaposition of a humid bamboo structure next to an anodyne skyscraper, on the periphery of Manhattan, enhances the singularity of the project.

The combination of water sprinklers with courtyard spotlights make the light covering appear much more solid.

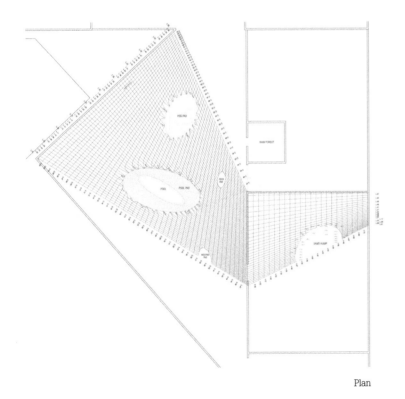

Plan

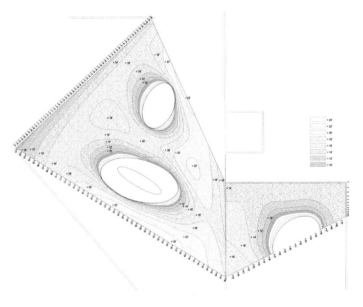

Topography

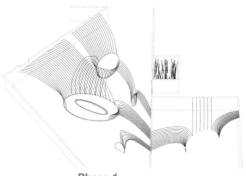

Phase 1

Phase 2

Construction phases

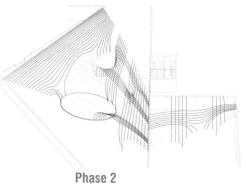

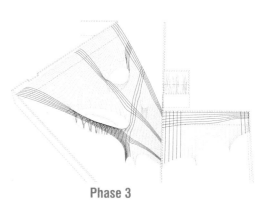

Phase 3

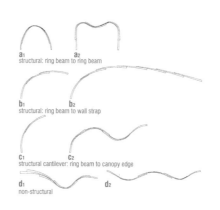

a₁ a₂
structural: ring beam to ring beam

b₁ b₂
structural: ring beam to wall strap

c₁ c₂
structural cantilever: ring beam to canopy edge

d₁
non-structural d₂

Splice types

The panoramic vision of the court-yard demonstrates the diverse spaces that can be created by using a traditional technique such as bamboo construction, which is yet to be explored by the vanguard.

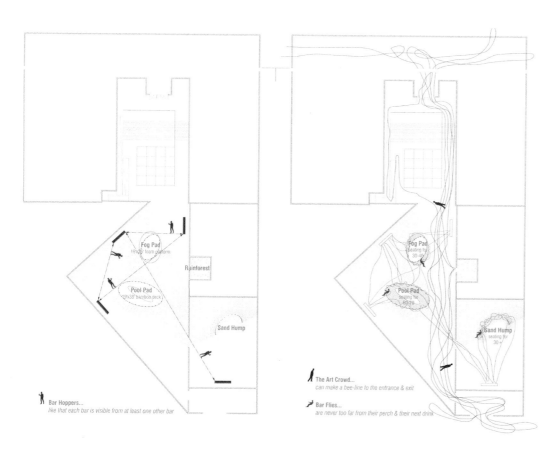

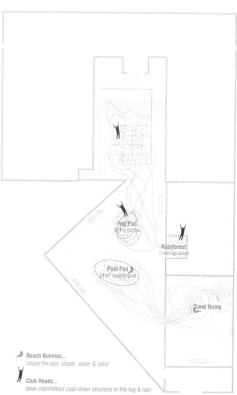

Bar Hoppers...
like that each bar is visible from at least one other bar

The Art Crowd...
can make a bee-line to the entrance & exit

Bar Flies...
are never too far from their perch & their next drink

Beach Bunnies...
chase the sun, shade, water & sand

Club Heads...
have intermittent cool-down sessions in the fog & rain

User diagrams

Audi

Architect: Klaus Schmidhuber

Address:
Schmidhuber and Partner
Nederlinger Strasse 21, 80638 Munich, Germany
+49 89 157 997
www.schmidhuber.de
info@schmidhuber.de

Fair: Motor Show 2005, Geneva, Switzerland
Other cities: No
Primary material: Plastic
Photos: © Andreas Keller

For the Audi stand in the car hall in Frankfurt, 2005, the idea was to raise a small platform to display the cars and give them center stage. The actual stand would be relegated to the parameter of two sides of the rectangular plot, creating an attractive L-shaped plan. On the short side, a two-story block was built that housed all the amenities, from the offices and storage to the restaurant, and which had a large terrace from which visitors could contemplate the vehicles. The long side featured four cubic display volumes, which alluded to the 25th anniversary of the Audi Quattro, one of the company's most emblematic models. The cubes hung from the ceiling from cables at a similar height to the second floor; their four faces acted as advertising boards. Beneath each cube were various elements that made reference to this vehicle's history; the space generated a cross of spatial planes and the viewer was placed in a point of four different atmospheres. Since the ceiling was conceived as a screen for showing promotional videos, the space emulated the feeling of being in a panoramic cinema, surrounded by images.

The color most associated with Audi is silver, and so a neutral tone was required which would not clash with this metallic color: White and gray were present in all the vertical elements, and orange appeared sporadically at the bottom of a wall or on the ceiling of the bar to enhance the predominant bright chromatics.

The large surface area of the pavilion was occupied by Audi's new models, leaving a central strip for showing the company's former emblematic models.

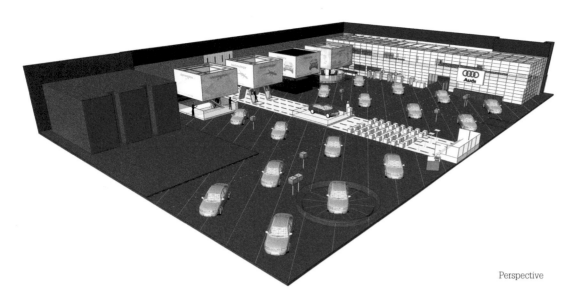

Perspective

Geschichte

25 Years quattro®

History

25 quattro

in 7 countries

19

1980   1984   1988   1991   1993   2001 2004

German

The video loop shown inside the four
small pavilions, which explained the
evolution of the Audi Quattro, created four different environments.

Formex

Architect: Marge

Address:
Marge Arkitecten
Repslagarg 15 A, 118 46 Stockholm, Sweden
+46 854 591 940
www.marge.se
info@marge.se

Fair: Formex, Stockholm, Sweden
Other cities: No
Primary material: Walls equipped with adjustable lighting
Photos: © Johan Fowelin, Magnus Skoglöf

During its 14-year history, the Formex fair, which specializes in gift items, design, and craftwork, has gained a name for itself as one of the most important fairs in Sweden. Given its character as a showcase for new trends that attracts a large audience, both professional and non-professional, the fair places a special emphasis on signalization and communication.

Marge was tasked with creating a stand that would serve as a visual reference and be able to accommodate a large number of visitors. In order to avoid long lines at the information desk, the architects opted to create a 4,300-square foot pavilion with a straightforward circulation system that designates the main access to the front area and the exit towards the remaining pavilions. This path diversifies at different points such as the lounge area, information desks, an exhibition hall, and various intermediate spaces with panels and other objects from the fair, generating varied points of interest and thus preventing congestion and creating a relaxed environment.

Rising above the information desk and exhibition hall, a glowing prism covered in white panels at first glance appears to be the second floor of the pavilion: in reality, the object functions as an advertisement, attracting attention from the public to the only poster without a name, brand, or symbol. This non-identity strategy allows the pavilion to be easily recognized and resolves through efficient and simple means two apparently contradictory functions: to provide an area for rapid circulation and to serve as a symbolic reference point.

The white light dominates the entire pavilion as the only distinguishable element, refusing to make any reference to a brand name. As a result, the pavilion stands out among the other constructions.

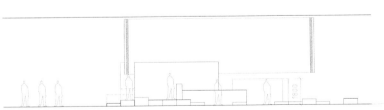

Section A

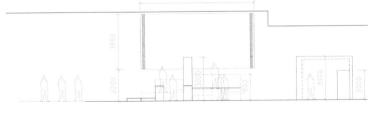

Section B

The white light by itself acts as a sign, helping to identify the fair organizers's pavilion as a neutral place, where all exhibitors are represented.

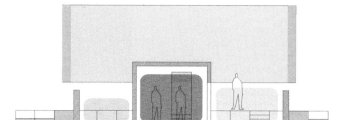

Section

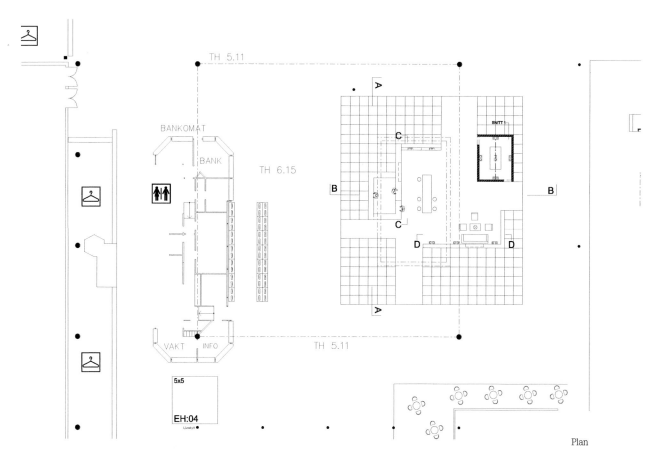

Plan

Urban Satellite Ektop-1

Architects: Pier Schneider, Franz Wunschel

Address:
    Exyzt
    69 Rue de Hauteville, 75010 Paris, France
        +33 146 079 004
www.exyzt.org
contact@exyzt.org

Fair: Nuit Blanche 2001, Paris, France
Other cities: Possibly
Primary material: Scaffoldings
Photos: © Sophie Robichon/Marie de Paris

The Nuit Blanche forms part of the Paris Town Council's cultural program and consists of various artistic performances and street parties throughout the evenings at the beginning of October. Since it began in 2001, the aim of the Nuit Blanche has been both to revitalize forgotten parts of Paris and to reinterpret well-known monuments, as Sophie Calle did with the Eiffel Tower.

As part of this cycle, the Exyzt group built a light structure in Les Halles, one of the city's busiest squares. The module took the shape of a satellite, and its three stories dominated the entire square. The idea proposed for the cultural program was to stage an alien spaceship landing on Earth and then investigating what was happening in the square. With the help of spotlights and cameras, passersby were filmed and the images were projected in real time on the façades of surrounding buildings.

In faculties of architecture the square of Les Halles is cited as one of the worst examples of urban planning in Europe, an opinion shared by residents of the center of Paris. The Exyzt group, with the help of spotlights and cameras, managed to revamp the appearance of this enclave. It went from being a fragmented space to an open one, where Parisians could see themselves reflected in the façades of the square, a kind of symbolic recovery of this space on behalf of the people.

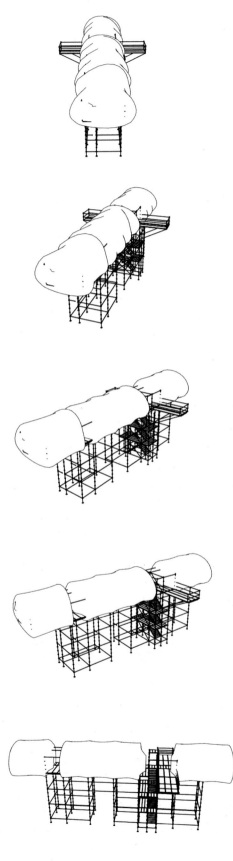

With the help of spotlights, the groups of people walking through the square of Les Halles could be picked out, while a video projector reproduced the images from the street on the façades of the square's buildings.

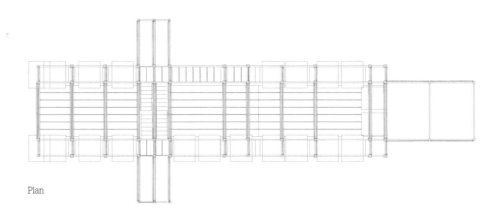

Plan

The scaffolding structure is very simple, allowing for quick assembly and dismantling without the need for heavy machinery.

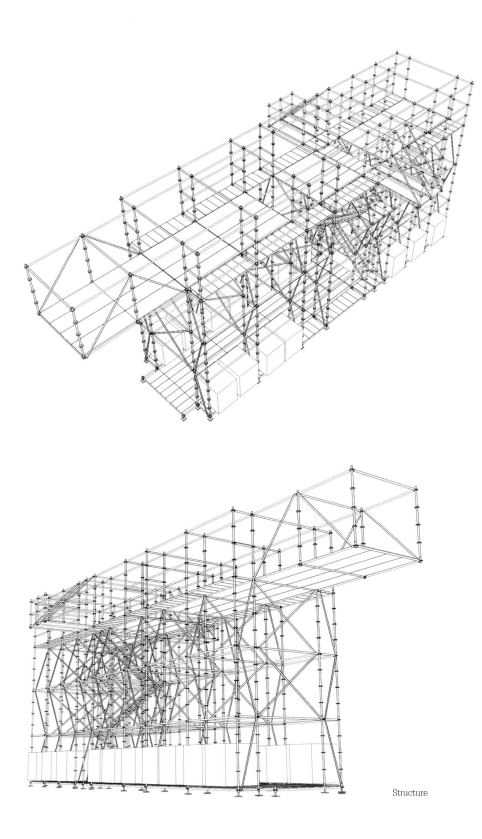

Structure

Only the top section of the scaffolding was covered in fabric, creating an image similar to that of a satellite. This was the effect the creators wanted.

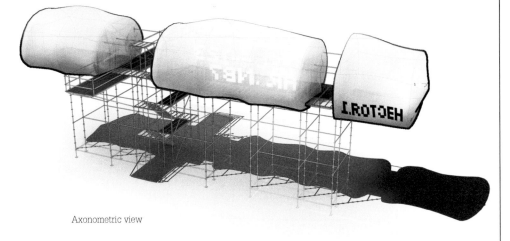

Axonometric view

Blur Building

Architects: Elizabeth Diller, Ricardo Scofidio

Address:
  Diller and Scofidio
  36 Cooper Square, 5F, New York, NY 10003, USA
        +1 2 122 607 971
www.dillerscofidio.com
disco@dillerscofidio.com

Fair: Swiss Expo 2002, Yverdon-les-Bains, Switzerland
Other cities: No
Primary material: Water
Photos: © Beat Widmer

The Blur building was one of the most admired of 2002 and will undoubtedly be featured in all architectural monographs in the twenty-first century. From a simple design, the architects Didlier and Scofidio constructed a building based on the limits of architecture and this century's need for visuals.

This structure, raised above Lake Neuchatel, uses the area's most common element for the leading role: water. With the help of pumps and a circuit of pipes and sprinklers, the building is constantly enshrouded in a large cloud of water, which changes depending on the wind, the humidity, or the temperature. These variables are all controlled by computer, so the effects, although always different, are minimally controlled. Its 1000-square yard surface can accommodate over 400 people, who upon entering lose all acoustic and visual reference points. Only the upper section houses a space that escapes the cloud of water; from this point one can contemplate the rain constantly falling over the lake. A bar was installed on the lower level, half submerged in water, where bottled water from different parts of the world can be tasted.

Although the Blur building can be interpreted as a dadaistic machine or as new and illogically Sisyphean, the architects' intention was to create a low-tech non-spectacular monument which showed nothing but the impossibility of seeing architecture.

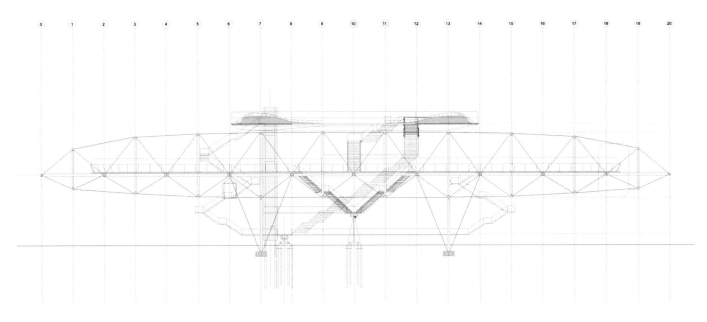

Section

The cloud of water, which creates an invisible pavilion in the middle of the lake, was the big attraction of the exhibition.

The long walkway was needed to put enough distance between the pavilion and the coast to achieve the desired weather-related effects.

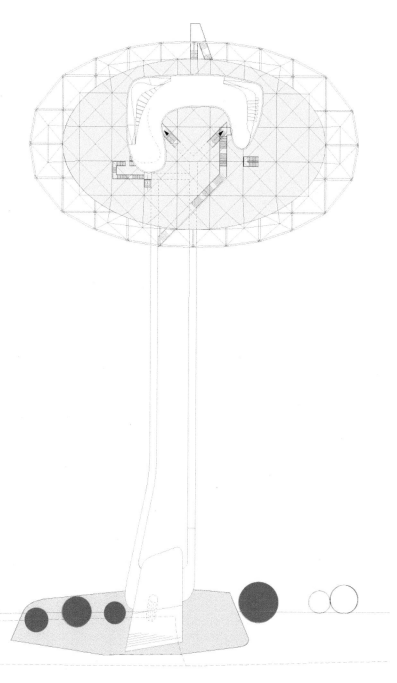

Plan

Given the instability of the lake floor, it was necessary to imbed very deep pile drives in order to safely support the structure.

Structure

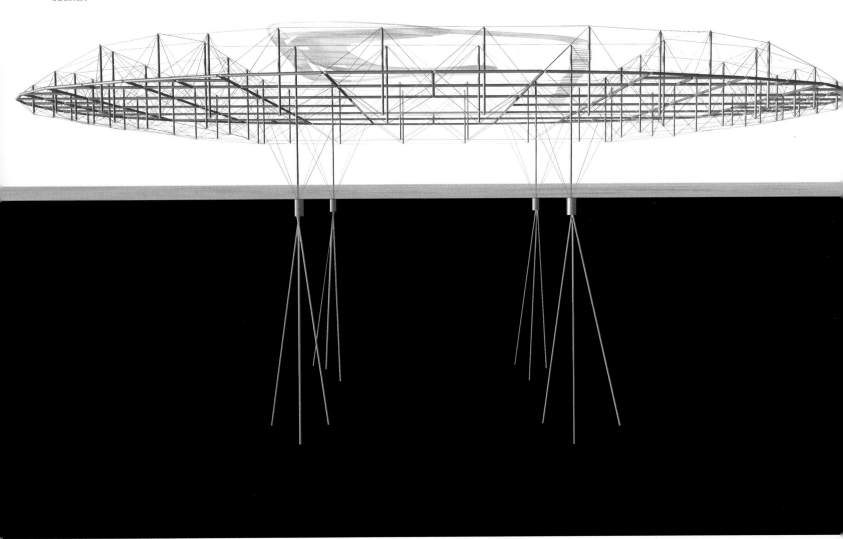

The different lights and the constant wind changes meant the pavilion never looked the same.

On the upper section of the pavilion, a space was raised which escaped the cloud of water, thereby allowing contemplation of the weather effects on the lake.

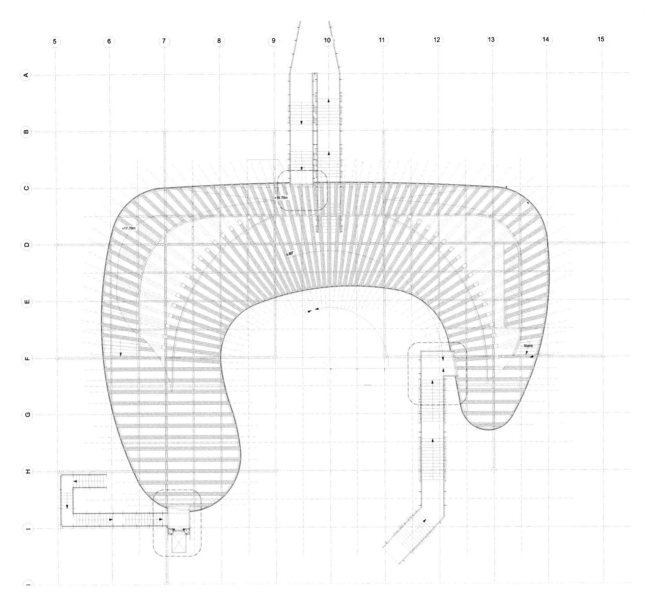

View point plan

The round shape of the upper platform and its different heights meant that there was always a point free of water, and it was, therefore, always able to function as a viewing platform.

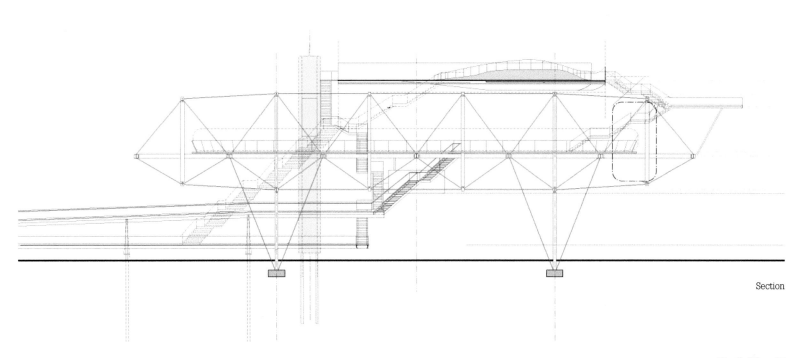

Section

Architect: Caramel, Friedrich Stiper

Address:
    Caramel
    Schottenfeldgasse 72/II/3, Vienna 1070, Austria
            +43 1 596 34 90
www.caramel.at
kha@caramel.at

Fair: K04, Düsseldorf, Germany
Other cities: Possibly
Primary material: Lightweight wood
Photos: © Caramel

The design of the AMI pavilion in the Düsseldorf trade fair is an effort to relieve the visitor from the over-stimulation normally experienced at this type of competitive arena. The idea was to create a peaceful atmosphere where visitors could relax. The form also had to refer to the company logo, seen in the triple "loop" and the color.

The initial idea was to isolate the inside of the stand. To do this a ribbon was designed that folded back on itself, creating a small interior space. Inside, the tables and televisions are arranged so that the visitor can sit comfortably on one of the chairs, which are built directly into the wall.

Depending on the viewing angle, the triple loop could appear either open or closed.

Each of the module's rings was formed from five prefabricated sections of light weight wood, which are easily assembled, allowing it to be reused and stored in a very short space of time. This is a valuable quality at trade fairs.

The comfort of the seats attached directly to the skin of the pavilion make this place ideal for rest.

The assembly is quick, as all the pieces are prefabricated and the three rings are put together in the same way every time.

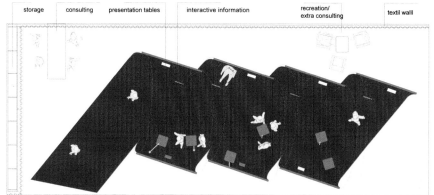

| storage | consulting | presentation tables | interactive information | recreation/ extra consulting | textil walll |

Plan

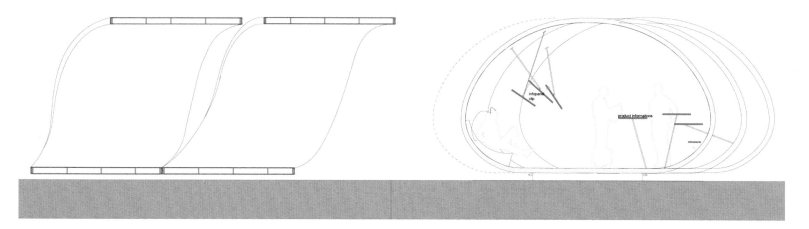

Sections

Depending on the angle of approach, the pavilion walls appear either continuous or permeable.

The similarity with the brand's logo, together with the simplicity and comfort of its assembly, mean this stand can be reused in different fairs and even for other events.

Tomihiro Art Museum

Architect: Makoto Yokomizo

Address:
AAT – Makoto Yokomizo Architects
4F Insatu Kaikan Bld., 4-1 Kikui-cho,
Shinjuku, 162-0044 Tokyo, Japan
    +81 332 059 580
www.aatplus.com
yoko@aatplus.com

Location: Tomihiro Art Museum, Gunma, Japan
Other cities: No
Primary material: Concrete
Photos: © Shiheru Ohno

The Tomihiro Museum is an architectural proposal, without schools of thought, which responds to the need to exhibit artist Tomihiro Hoshiro's work in one of Japan's most popular museums.

The project moves away from neutral exhibition spaces such as London's White Cube gallery or extensible projects like the proposal for Le Corbusier in 1931 for a contemporary art center in Paris. In contrast to today's trend, the architects wanted to create a space without hierarchy, appearing as a mass of soap bubbles, where each bubble has access to those around it, thereby giving rise to multiple connections. The spheres' diameter, the color of the walls, and the lighting, create rooms, which in turn become more intimate as they approach the center of the structure.

Despite the proposal of a round shape on top of a square one, the influence of Mies van der Rohe's National Gallery in Berlin is evident here. The result, however, is fruit of a different architectural proposition.

The connections between the round rooms create a continual space throughout the museum, while at the same time each room offers something different.

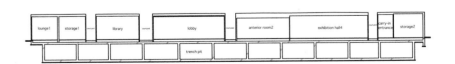

| lounge1 | storage1 | | library | | lobby | | anterior room2 | exhibition hall4 | | carry-in entrance | storage2 |

trench pit

Section

Working with a variety of circumferences throughout the spaces gave the interior a high level of fluidity, and allowed a complex problem to be solved with a simple solution.

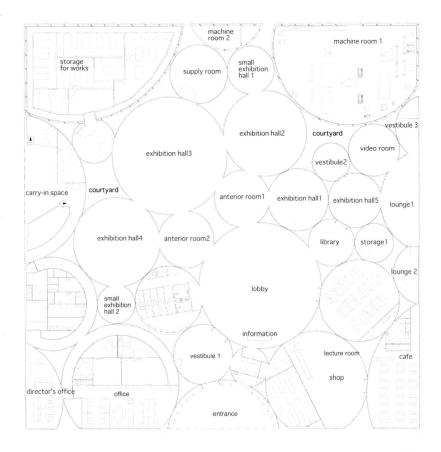

storage for works

machine room 2

machine room 1

supply room

small exhibition hall 1

exhibition hall2

courtyard

vestibule 3

video room

exhibition hall3

vestibule2

carry-in space

courtyard

anterior room1

exhibition hall1

exhibition hall5

lounge1

exhibition hall4

anterior room2

library

storage1

lounge 2

lobby

small exhibition hall 2

information

vestibule 1

lecture room

cafe

shop

director's office

office

entrance

Plan

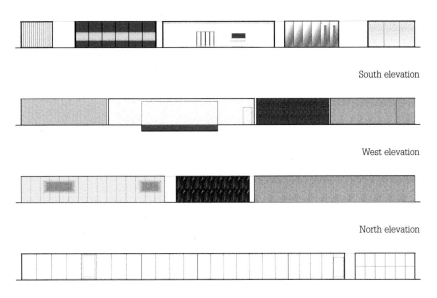

South elevation

West elevation

North elevation

East elevation

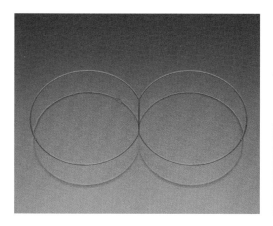 

The joining of two circumferences occurs naturally in nature, as much in physics as in living creatures.

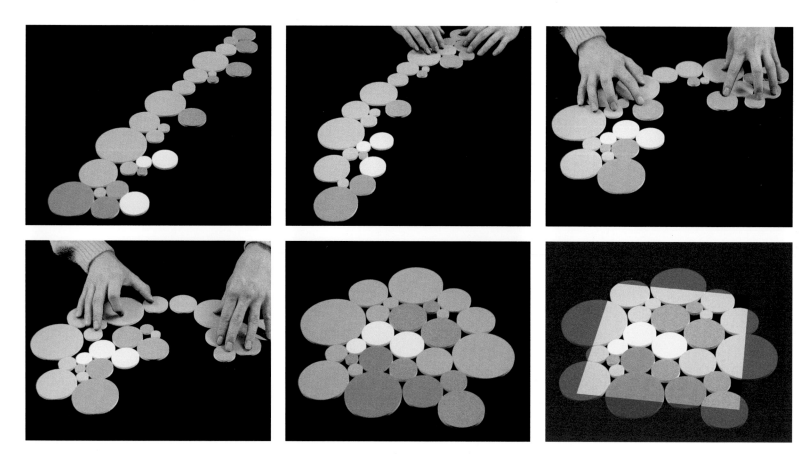

The scale-model of the building, without its roof, gives an idea of the project's dimensions.

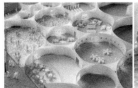

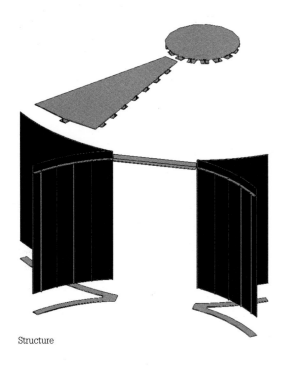

Structure

The exhibit was built from prefabricated pieces, allowing it to be assembled directly on site.

The different openings allowed for very different types of light: the small circular openings in the walls stand out as a unique solution in the world of architecture, creating a very soft light.

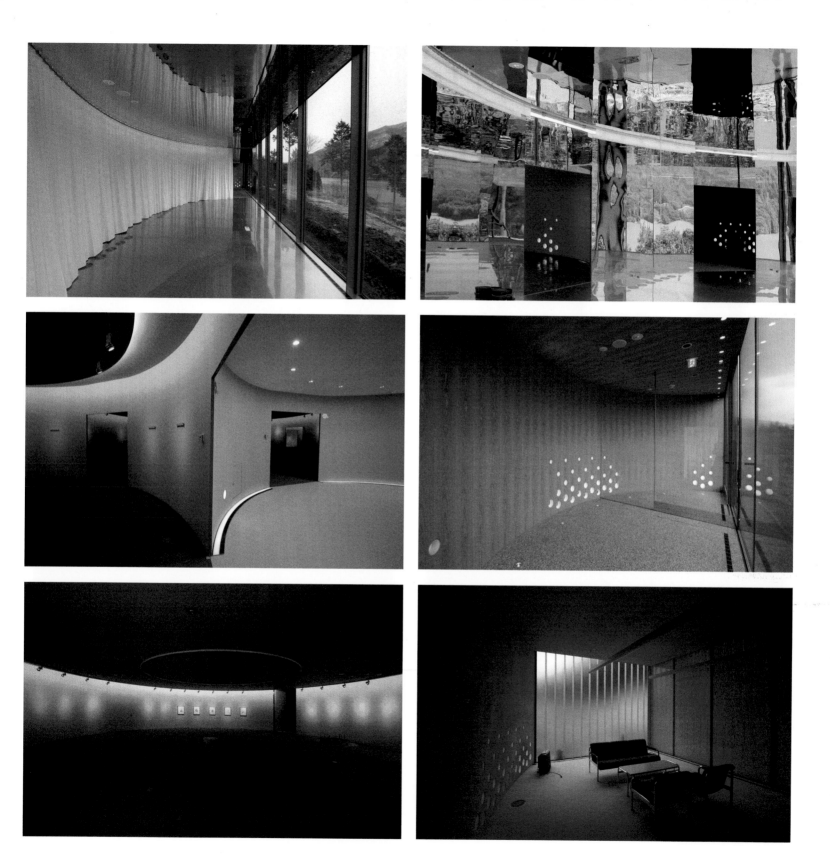

The view from the bar of the surrounding landscape explains why the route around the museum finishes here, in this rich space, where the purest geometric shapes mix with nature.

Tramo

Architect: Francesc Rifé

Address:
   Rife Design
   Escoles Pies 25, 08017 Barcelona, Spain
      +34 934 141 288
www.rife-design.com
f@rife-design.com

Fair: Feria Internacional del Mueble 2005, Valencia, Spain
Other cities: No
Primary material: Glass and stained wood
Photos: © Eugeni Pons

The furniture made by Tramo is considered, among interior design professionals, to be the best on the market. Their modular systems and high-quality finishes give good results in offices and shops as well as in homes.

For Valencia's trade fair, a neutral stand was designed which gave the leading role to the product: a large box with its two lateral sides open to the public and glass walls, like a shop window, on the front side. The glass wall acted as an eye-catching division from the rest of the trade fair, although at the same time its transparency made it very accessible. On display behind the glass, on dark bases, were different items of furniture lit by soft coral light as if in a museum. The objects thus acquired prestige in the eyes of the visitors, while inside the pavilion the same products were laid out on the floor.

A large, black, wooden frieze, which gives the stand an air of seriousness and quality, dominated the outside of the pavilion. This dark color was repeated inside, creating a contrast with the light wood of the floor.

Leaving the sides open facilitated the circulation inside, inviting visitors to enter.

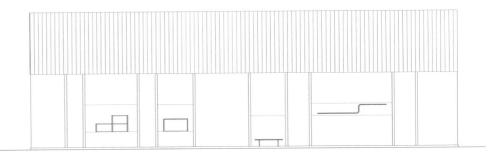

Elevation

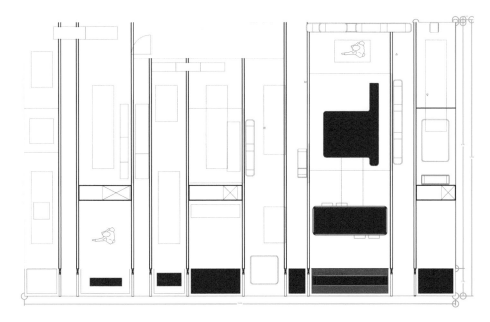

Plan

Rendering

The strong presence of the brand's products made the architects choose a neutral presentation setting, putting the spotlight on the furniture.

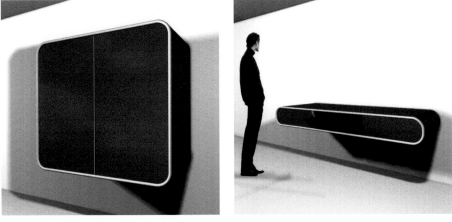

Viabizzuno

Architect: Upo Architettura/Viabizzuno

Address:
Viabizzuno
10 Via Romagnoli, 40010 Bentivoglio, Italy
    +39 05 1890 8011
www.viabizzuno.com
viabizzuno@viabizzuno.com

Fair: Interlight 2005, Moscow, Russia
Other cities: No
Primary material: *Riposalibri* module
Photos: © Viabizzuno

Viabizzuno is an interior design and furniture studio that stands out, above all, for the excellence of their lighting solutions. At the Moscow trade fair they exhibited just one of their most exquisite pieces, the Doccia Goccia, a transparent shower with a lighting system incorporated into the water outlet. This object was in the center of the stand, half-hidden by two dividing modules, as if it were the only object on display. This arrangement helped enhance the mystery of the piece, since from the outside it was not possible to determine what this great glass bubble was used for. Once in the stand, the visitor was able to see that the dividing modules were also Viabizzuno products: the small modules acted as classifiers, but thanks to the ease with which they could be joined, could also be used as shelving. The confrontation of the two products and the strategy of hiding one behind the other highlighted the versatility of the company, which can always provide elegant solutions for both the most exquisite and the most functional pieces.

On the last days of the fair, clients were given a classifier, meaning the stand was slowly dismantled. As well as pleasing the clients, this gesture helped with the break down of the stand and meant a lighter return home.

The Viabizzuno pavilion was built from a design from the same company, *Riposalibri*, that functions here as a wall.

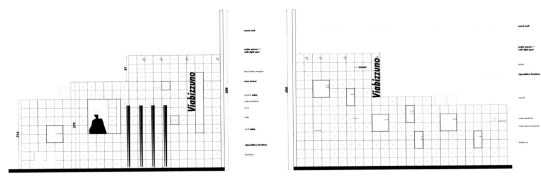

Elevations

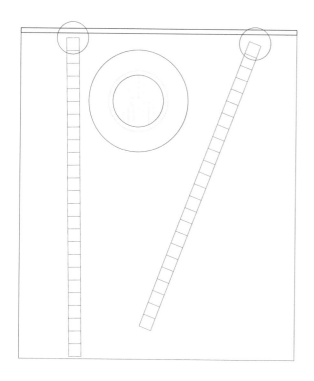

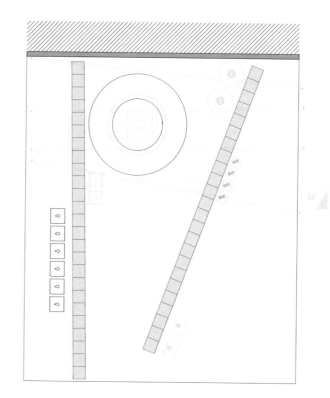

Plans

Using the same module meant the construction and dismantling was very simple, and also allowed windows to be opened when needed.

The module was used both as a wall and as shelving to display other products of the brand.

Inside the pavilion one of the most exquisite designs is on display: a shower with cenital lighting incorporated.

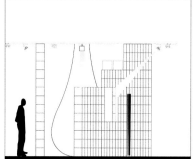

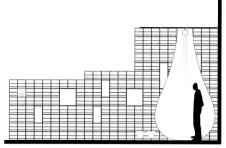

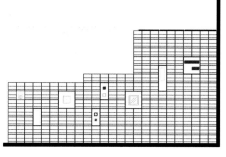

Sections

Forbo

Architect: Concrete

Address:
Concrete Architectural Asociates
Rozengracht 133, III, 1016 LV Amsterdam, Netherlands
+31 205 200 200
www.concrete.archined.nl
info@concrete.archined.nl

Location: Forbo showroom, Assendelft, Netherlands
Other cities: No
Primary material: Steel Moëbius Loop
Photos: © Concrete Architectural Associates

This international flooring company is known for having the widest range of products in the market. Its new showroom in Assendelft had to provide space for displaying the majority of its collection, but the vertical surface area was insufficient despite the space measuring almost 600 square yards.

One of the solutions considered was to compartmentalize the building into small hexagonal rooms, since this shape could be identified with the brand's logo and would also have made exhibiting the product easier. It was rejected, however, as the image of a labyrinth was not appropriate to a showroom, which being multi-purpose, had to adapt to all kinds of events.

The idea of the Moebius ribbon finally emerged: a figure, which apart from being attractive, also represents infinity. The architects made three large steel ribbons, each around thirty feet long and nine feet wide, on which different collections of the company's product were mounted. Thanks to this elegant exhibition formula, it also showed how the products adapted to curved surfaces, and left the space free of any dividing features.

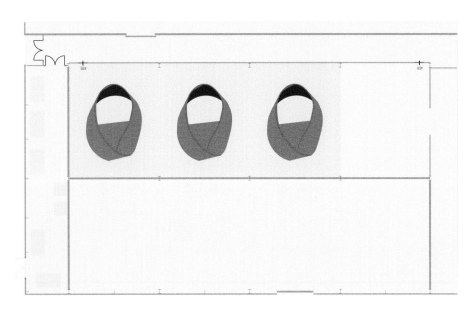

Plan

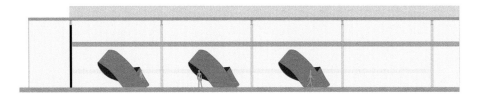

Sections

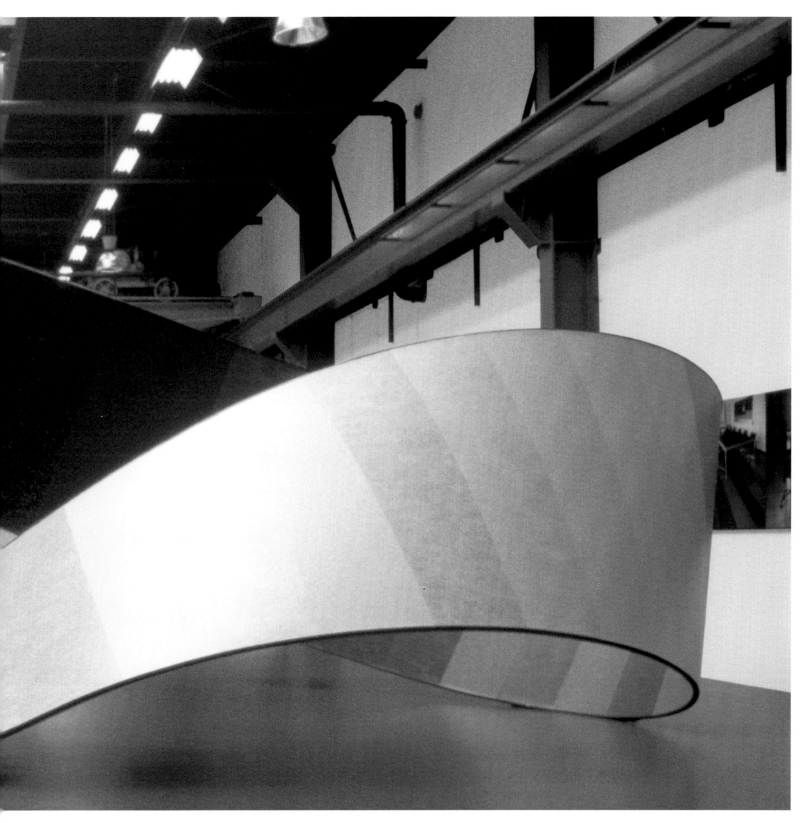

Comex

Architects: Jorge Hernández de la Garza, Gerardo Broissin

Address:
   BH – Broissin y Hernández de la Garza
   Misión de San Javier 65, 53130, México DF, México
         +52 555 344 2896
www.grupobh.com
info@broissinyhernandezdelagarza.com

Fair: Expo Cihac 2005
Other cities: No
Primary material: Resin
Photos: © Paul Czitrom

The paint company Comex wanted to appear in the Expo Chiac trade fair organized in Mexico DF with an innovative image and a pavilion that portrayed its investment in new products. The architects designed a large two-story aerodynamic volume, whose shapes allude to high-tech products like planes and luxury cars. The upper and lower sections of the main façade fold inwards, and where they meet marks the division between floors. This gives the project unity and allows the bottom floor to be completely open to the public, while the upper floor, which is more closed, was reserved as a space for meetings with clients. Illuminated panels advertising the products were positioned on the walls of the upper floor.

The pavilion was made from a white resin, chosen for its ductility, the quality it gives the finishes, and because it allows the panels to stand out as the main feature. The second floor, a more relaxed zone, provides interesting views of the trade fair.

The base ring used for the pavilion was chosen for its constructive logic and for the ease with which it can be industrially fabricated.

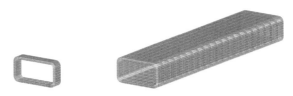
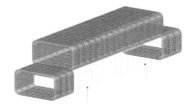

The finish of neutral colors gave the pavilion an image of modernity and simplicity, which was praised throughout the fair.

Structure process

The opening in the center of the stand allowed large numbers of visitors to circulate, and facilitated the work of the stewardesses.

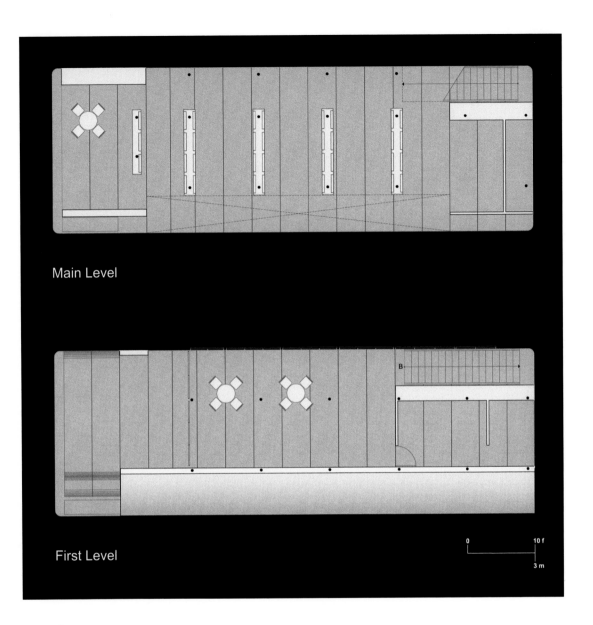

Main Level

First Level

0   10 f
3 m

The second floor was inaccessible for the majority of the public, so it served as an office and a place of rest.

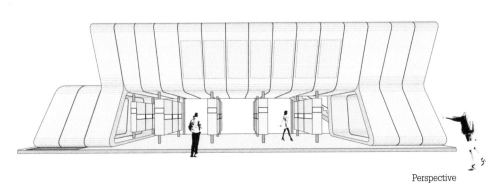

Perspective

The vanguard image the client desired was resolved in such a striking and appropriate way that even the paint pots seemed like new objects.

The round shape of the pavilion seemed to float, as there was no contact between the structure and the floor.

Count-it

Architect: Maurice Mentjens

Address:
  Maurice Mentjens Design
  Martinusstraat 20, 6123 BS Holtum, Netherlands
      +31 464 811 405
www.mauricementjens.com
info@mauricementjens.com

Fair: Highlife in Utrecht 2002, Highlife in Amsterdam 2003,
Netherlands
Other cities: Basel
Primary material: Matt plexiglass tubes
Photos: © Bert Jansse

Despite a low budget and small size, the Count-it stand in the
2005 trade fairs was made as eye-catching as possible. The
solution most commonly used toward this end is the applica-
tion of striking colors, but in this case the process was invert-
ed and white was chosen as the distinguishing element. The
company also wanted to employ a typology which contrasted
with those normally used in fairs: instead of an open architecture, the image of a cell was used, with thick bars that delin-
eated the space.

The surprise of the visitors was guaranteed, since in the midst
of the monotony of colors Count-it was the only space which
was apparently neutral and closed in the entire arena. Once
past the initial impression, the bars revealed themselves as
curtains which could be parted, giving access to the central
information space.

The pavilion can be easily assembled and dismantled, and consists of mass-produced elements. This means it can be assembled as much as is required, and also that the initial configura-
tion can be modified.

Since it is made from different pieces, this pavilion can be easily adapted to different spaces.

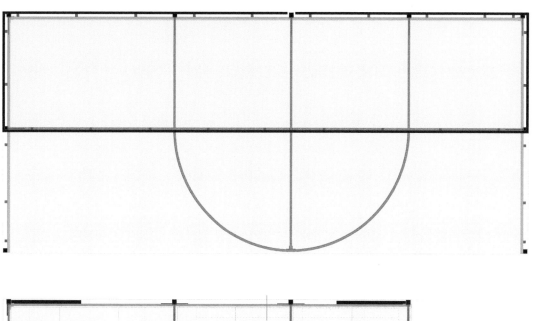

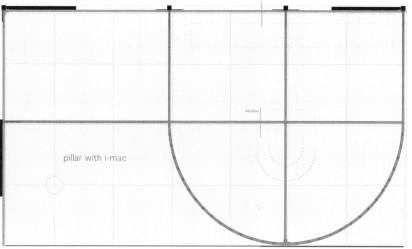

pillar with i-mac

4420mm

Plans

The plan layout aids its assembly, as well as assuring that the resulting stand always produces an ordered and well-proportioned image.

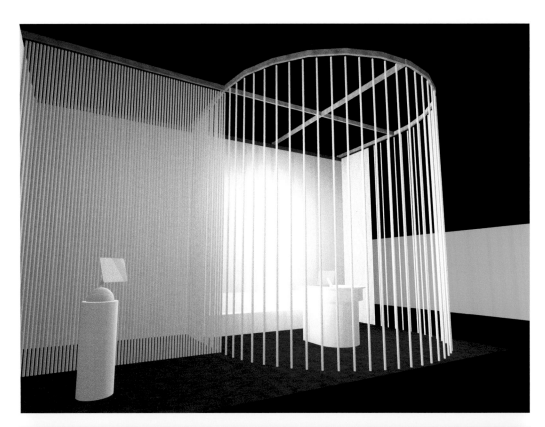

Since they are not attached to the floor, what appear to be bars of a cage instead act as a curtain, making it easy it enter or leave the stand.

Render

Institutional Prosthesis

Architect: Santiago Cirugeda

Address:
Recetas Urbanas
Joaquin Costa 7, 41002 Sevilla, Spain
+34 954 904 581
www.recetasurbanas.net
sc@recetasurbanas.net

Location: Espai d'Art Contemporani de Castelló,
Castellón de la Plana, Spain
Other cities: Possibly
Primary material: Plastic box formwork
Photos: © Recetas Urbanas

Santiago Cirugeda's installation responds to the need to modernize Castellón's Contemporary Art Museum building and adapt it to modern use. The artist designed a volume attached to the main building that broadens the museum's functions to encompass various pedagogical programs and provide it with a space for contemporary art. The city's different institutions may also make use of the two rooms for their respective cultural activities. This profile positions the museum at the forefront of the newest art centers in Europe, alongside Paris's Tokyo Palace or Barcelona's Macba, all of which operate under the premise that museums are active institutions available for the public to use.

The extension also created access to two large and previously inaccessible terraces. The peculiar vision of this artist and architect has filled this project with the profession's cynical elements, like a walkway that leads nowhere—possibly a reference to the first Koolhaas—or structural elements that find support from the walls, when the floor would be the most logical option. The exterior finish is also a gesture, critical of architects' concern for finding interesting textures that merely act as a media ploy. In this case, the "interesting texture" is made from slab formwork, one of the more economic construction materials. Here it is used to make journalists focus on the building without interfering with the work being done inside.

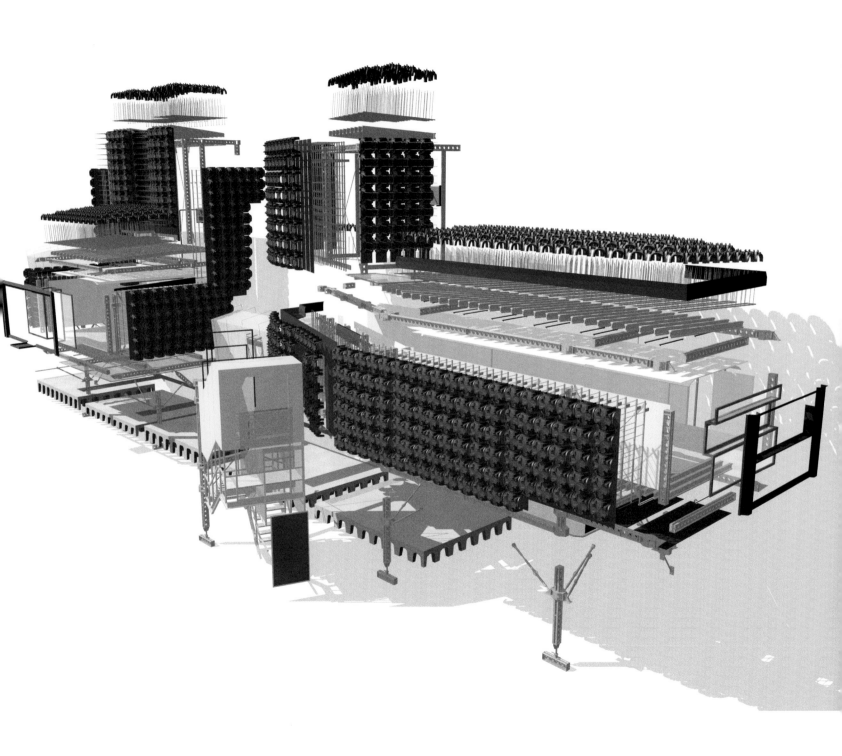

The appearance of the two modules on the Castellón landscape has changed the museum's image, making it visually bizarre but much more open to the public.

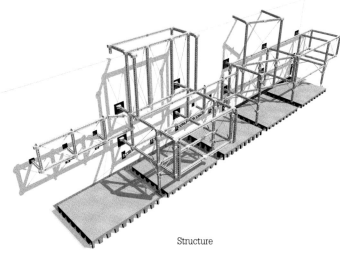

Structure

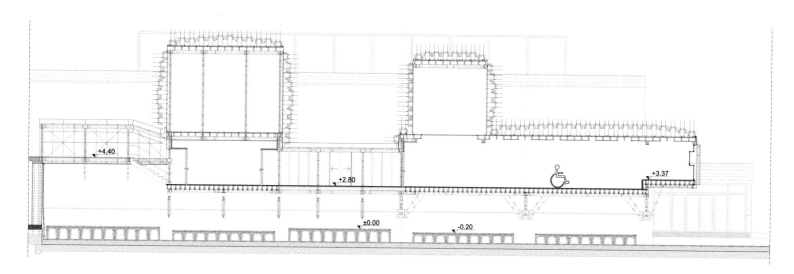

+4.40

+2.80

+3.37

±0.00   -0.20

Section

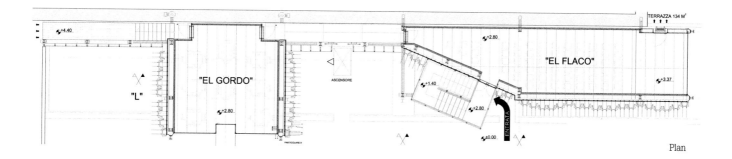

+4.40

TERRAZZA 134 M²

+2.80

"EL FLACO"

+3.37

"EL GORDO"

ASCENSORE

+1.40

+2.80

"L"

+2.80

ENTRATA

±0.00

PARTICOLARE 3

Plan

The cross-section of the Prosthesis shows how the walls of the building directly support the ephemeral structure. The two rooms and the walkways between them, leading to the terraces, can be seen from the plan.

The prosthesis is a structure that visually imposes itself on the surrounding urban landscape, and acts as an organizing feature for a new city square.

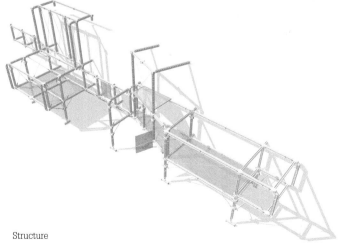

Structure

The large glass front gives light to the inside, and softens the hard image of the formwork and the steel rods.

The yellow of the stairs stands out as much from the white walls as from the black formwork. Highlighting the access in this way and leaving certain sections open emphasizes the museum's easy access.

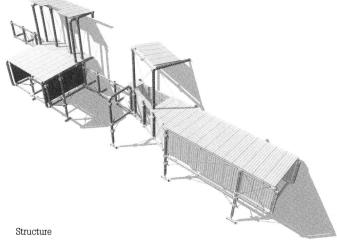

Structure

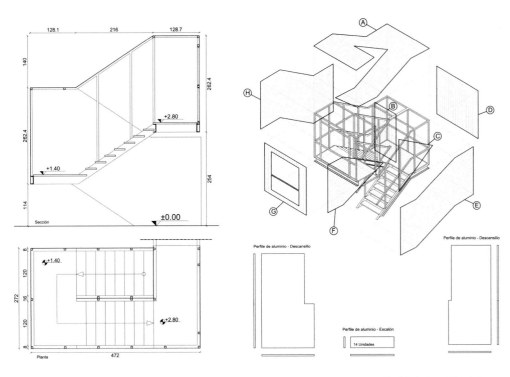

The fragmentation of the ephemeral structure's pieces was useful for the assembly, but also play a didactic and informative role, illustrating how the pavilion was constructed.

Exploted view of the staircase

Staircase structure

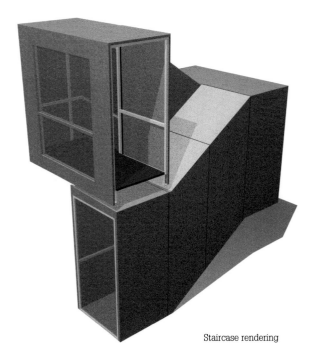

Staircase rendering

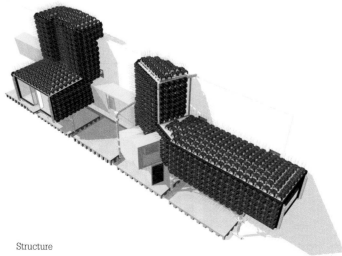

Structure

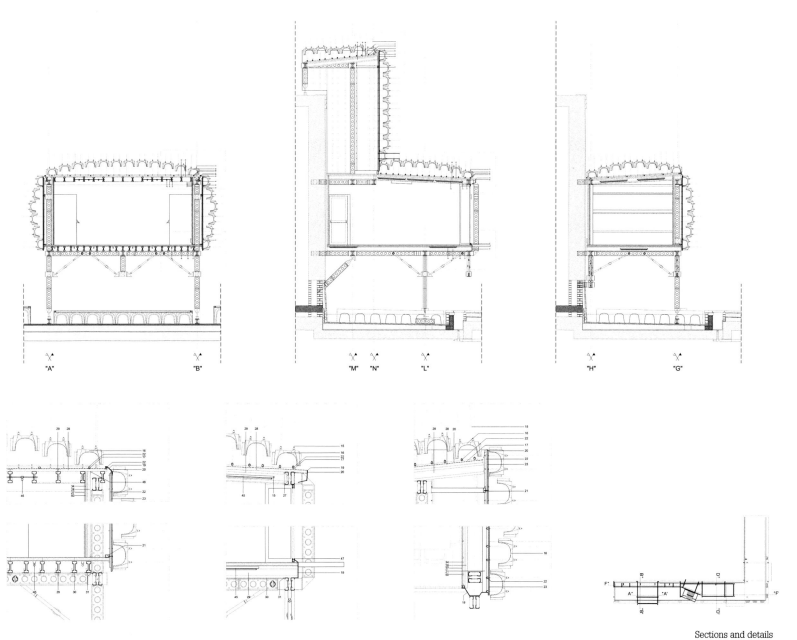

Sections and details

Serpentine Gallery Pavilion

Architects: Alvaro Siza, Eduardo Souto de Moura

Address:
   Souto de Moura
   Rua Aleixo 53 1º A, 4150-043 Porto, Portugal
       +351 22 610 8092
souto.moura@mail.telepac.pt

Place: Serpentine Gallery, Kensington Gardens, London
Other Cities: No
Primary material: Wood
Photo: © Tiago Figuereido, Studio Souto Moura

Each year London's Serpentine Gallery, located in Kensington Gardens, commissions renowned architects with the project of a summer pavilion for the area surrounding the gallery.

The Portuguese architects Alvaro Siza and Eduardo Soto de Moura worked with the idea of creating a structure that, from the outside, resembled a camping tent, focusing especially on the interaction between this and the neoclassical building of the gallery. The pavilion's reticular framework is composed of wooden beams which act as pillars and support for the roof; translucent plastic planks cover the structure's mesh, generating a single covering that appears to be a textile material.

Another key feature in the design was the adaptation of a geometric shape to the natural surroundings. The plan shows how the pavilion's nearly square floor is hidden beneath the free form of the roof, which stretches towards the trees, integrating perfectly with the environment.

The high-quality, elegant volume harmonizes with the classical gallery building. For this reason it is one of the greatest achievements of contemporary architecture.

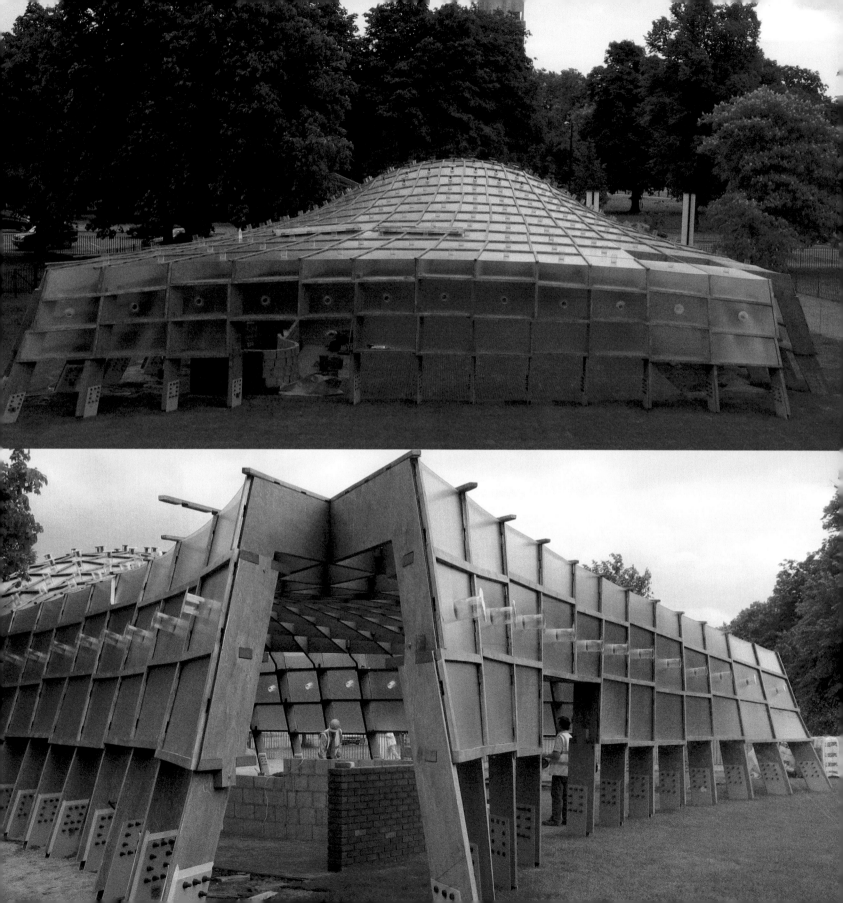

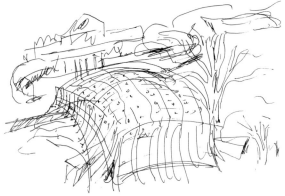

Sketches

The juxtaposition between buildings of different eras in a natural park is one of the most studied subjects in architecture today.

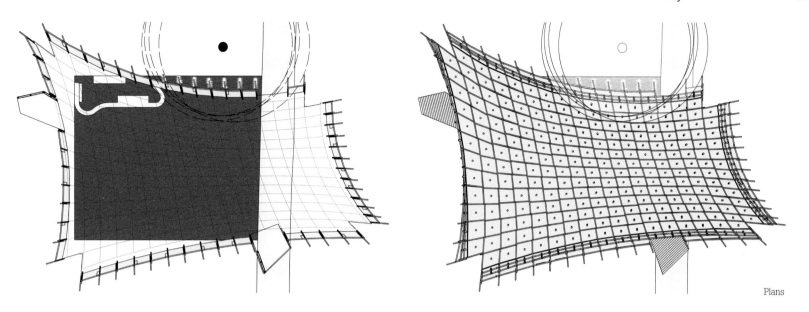

Plans

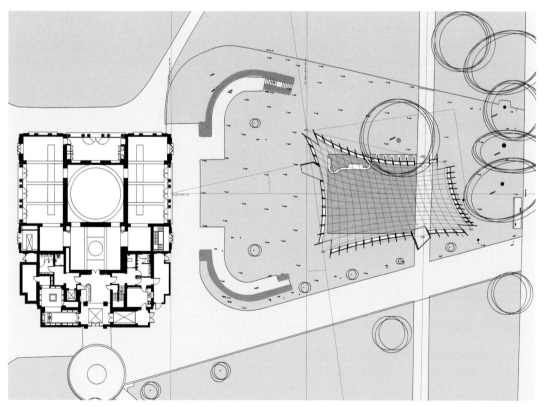

Situation plan

Spanish Pavilion Aichi 2005

Architects: Farshid Moussavi, Alejandro Zaera-Polo

Address:
  FOA – Foreign Office Architects
  55 Curtain Road, EC2A 3PT London, United Kingdom
    +44 20 7033 9800
www.f-o-a.net
mail@f-o-a.net

Fair: Expo 2005, Aichi, Japan
Other cities: No
Primary material: Octogonal glazed ceramic pieces
Photos: © Satoru Mishima

One of the international challenges of the twenty-first century is improving the productive relationship between different cultures, especially between East and West. Using this idea the FOA team sought to apply cultural fusion to architecture, and achieved this using research carried out into traditional Spanish architecture.

Architectural elements that filter light are present in gothic European architecture as well as Arabic, Japanese, and Southeast Asian. However, in the south of Spain, the mix of Christian and Arabic traditions gave rise to the fascinating lattice. It was precisely the study of these lattices that lead the architects to create the modular element used on the façade of the Spanish pavilion in Aichi's Universal Exhibition: six hexagonal pieces were designed which can be assembled in different ways without ever repeating the same pattern. They were fabricated using a glazed ceramic technique, common to the Mediterranean and Japan, and this was how the pavilion wall was built, giving it the appearance of a multicolor panel.

The adaptation of traditional architecture to modern construction techniques and the fusion of architectural concepts from different cultures made this pavilion the most admired feature of the exhibition. The visitors were impressed by its peculiar chromatics, and the architects were surprised that a hybrid object could have such an interesting outcome.

The powerful image of its continual wall, achieved through the colored hexagons, made the Spanish pavilion the most admired of the fair.

The apparent cartesianism on the outside was transformed into spaces of oblique shapes in the rooms inside, where the exterior's straight lines cannot be seen.

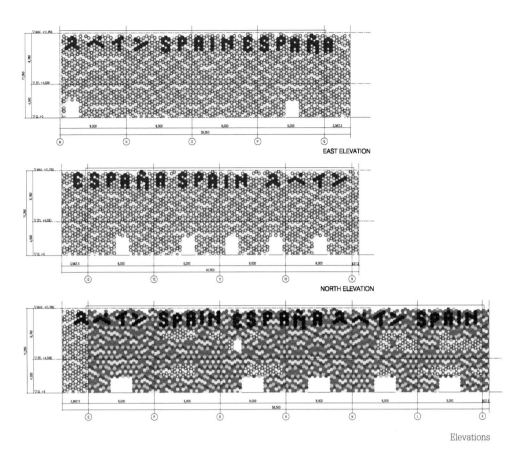

EAST ELEVATION

NORTH ELEVATION

Elevations

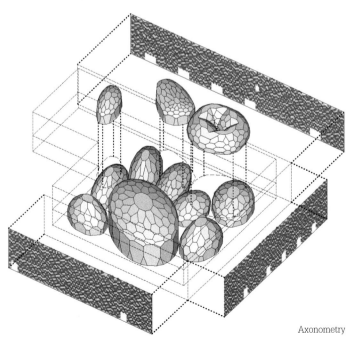

Axonometry

The inside rooms also employed the hexagons to generate spaces, as well as to form the display panels.

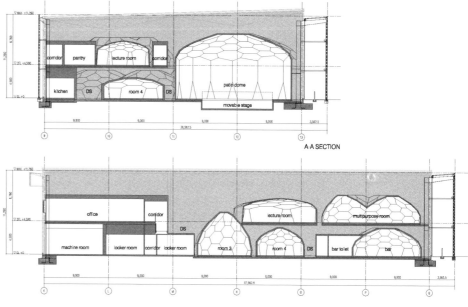

A-A SECTION

Sections

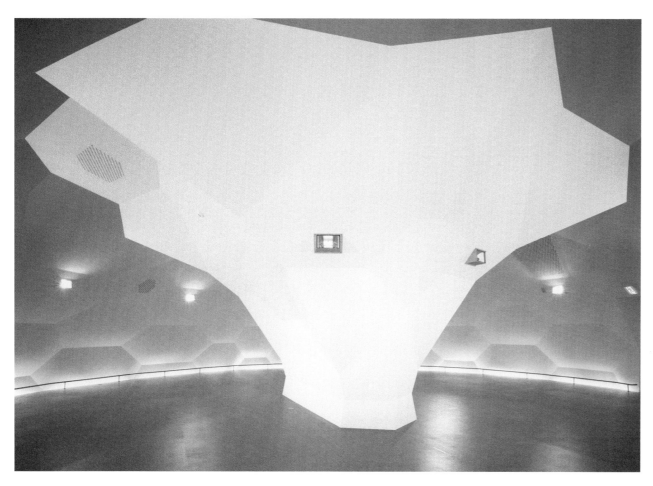

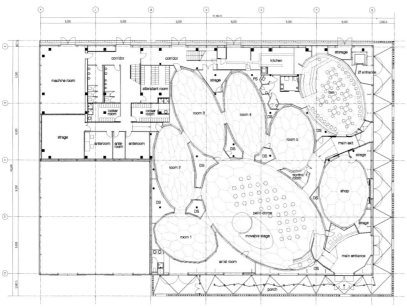

Plan

The interior complex was inspired by the richness of traditional Spanish architecture, where some rooms display an elaborate baroque style while others show a Cistercian simplicity.

Ibercon

Architect: Jordi Badia

Address:
  BAAS
  Frederic Rahola 63, 08032 Barcelona, Spain
        +34 933 580 111
www.jordibadia.com
info@jordibadia.com

Fair: SIMA 2004, Madrid, Spain
Other cities: Possibly
Primary material: Untreated rope
Photos: © Eugeni Pons

The BAAS studio's proposal for the Ibercon stand in the Property Hall in Madrid, 2004 called for using an unusual material to create a unique space that stands out above the rest of the exhibition stands. They wanted an economical design which was easy to store, could be reused, and which transmitted an image of elegance and simplicity.

The stand was devised as a continuous plane of ropes that filled in the ceiling, the walls, and the display stand. This idea required the fabrication of an iron frame on which the ropes were pulled taught. A dark carpet that covers the floor and the end of the stand complements the space.

Inside, three scale-models were installed and the plans of the construction company's buildings were exhibited on a foam panel, taking great care not to allow these materials to diminish the visual impact of the ropes. The interior was finished with classic furnishings of natural materials: chairs of light wood and sisal, and lamps made of wood laminated with Coderch. In contrast the table was dark, like the background furniture, and included a small fridge and storage space. The innovative work in this pavilion pleased the clients enormously, who had previous experience with these architects for their office block.

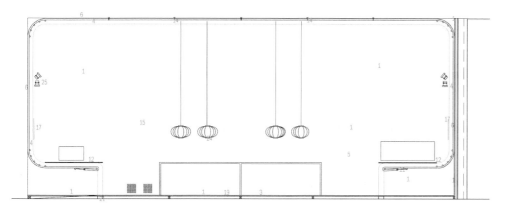

Frontal elevation

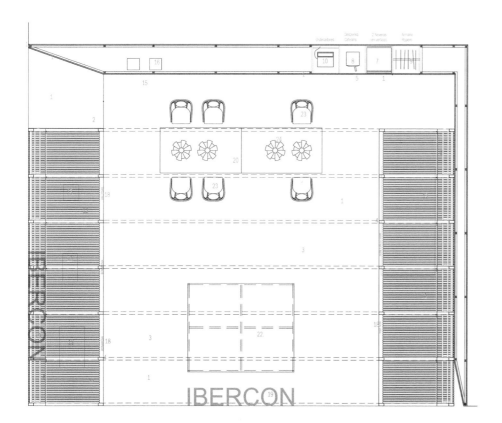

Plan

This project's simplicity, both in the plan and the assembly, shows how a good idea can generate functional, useful, and comfortable architecture.

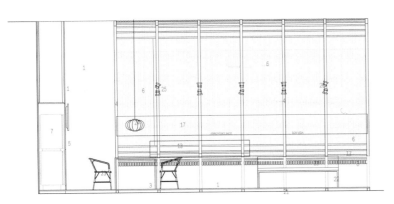

Longitudinal section

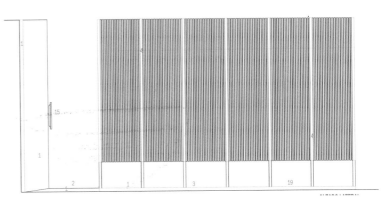

Side elevation

Rope is a simple and cheap material that, if appropriately treated, can create a solid enclosure.

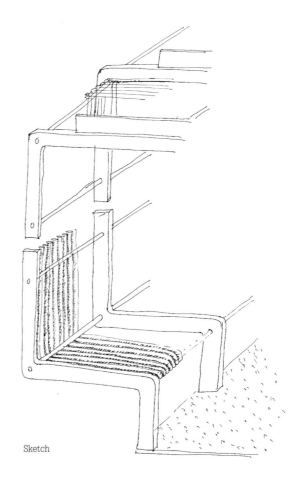

Sketch

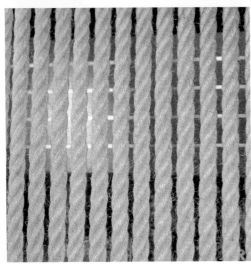

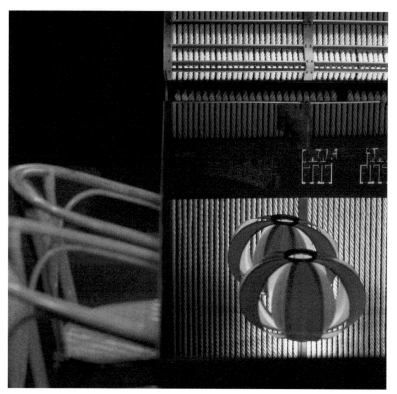

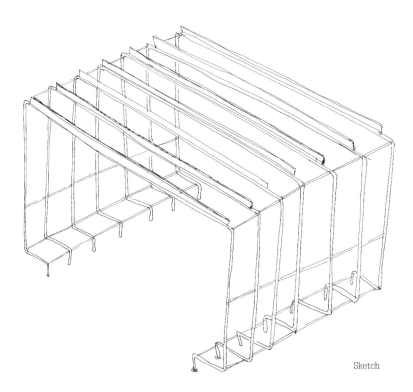

Sketch

The appropriate lighting gave the stand the desired atmosphere for the clients, who were more interested in having a good meeting space than one to display the products

Trinkbaunnen

Architects: Ernst J. Fuchs, Marie-Therese Harnoncourt

Address:
The Next Enterprise
Ausstellungsstrasse 5/2, 1020 Vienna, Austria
+43 17 296 388
www.thenextenterprise.at
office@thenextenterprise.at

Fair: Höfefest, Street Festival in St. Pölten, Austria
Other cities: Possibly
Primary material: Plastic
Photos: © The Next Enterprise

The "trinkbaunnen"—literally "drinking fountain"—is a huge refrigerator which can be used to offer fresh drinks anywhere in the city: all it needs for its installation is a water outlet and a power point. It was designed for the St. Pölten art festival with the idea of being reused as many times as necessary. Because it is inflatable, it can be stored in a very small space. It was also designed to be as independent from any form of infrastructure as possible, and it can be fed electricity from a small independent generator. After this, finding a water outlet in Austria, one of the wettest regions in Europe, presents no problem at all.

This volume of organic shapes works like a bar; it inflates with water and deposits the drinks in an internal cavity where they are cooled in a matter of hours. The constant circulation of water makes this great bar move slowly, like a caterpillar, lending it both a curious and fun quality. Despite its black color, it attracts the attention of both children and adults alike, and its large dimensions visibly modify the appearance of wherever it is installed. It is not simply a vending machine, but an attractive urban feature, which can be set up for reunions or meetings: Its mass makes it stand out although it is low enough not to interfere in any urban landscape. Its ability to adapt to and transform any space makes it a highly useful landscaping object.

This bizarre-looking inflatable bar can be installed in any public square.

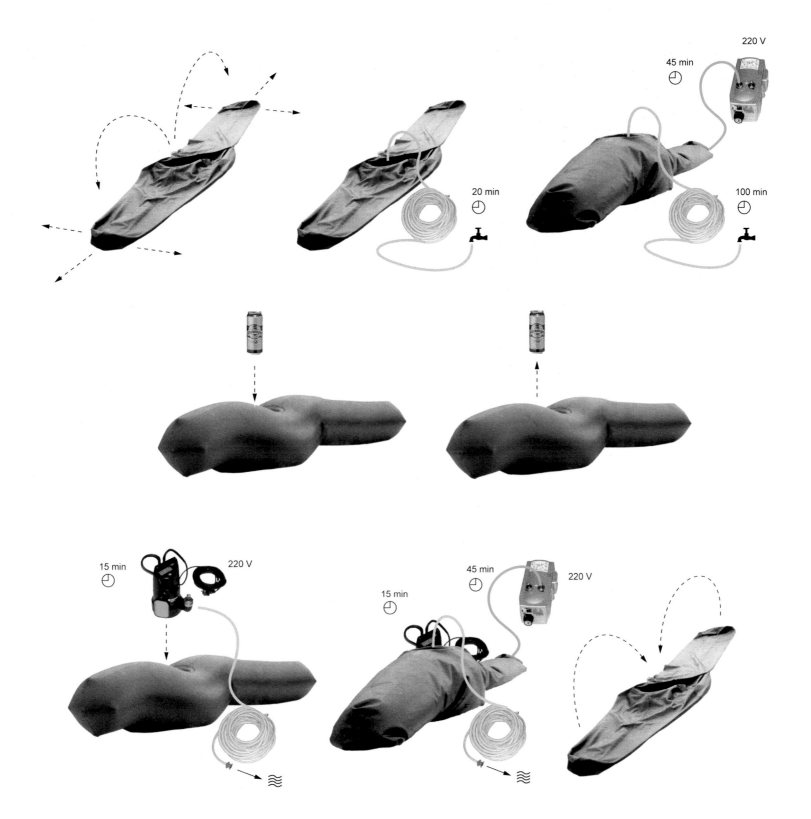

The ergonomic lines of the Trink-
bauten make it a comfortable object
and allow people to reach the drinks
from different points.

Apart from drawing attention because of its strange appearance, the line that it traces across the urban landscape generates a social gathering space.

Architects: Exyzt

Address:
Exyzt
69 Rue de Hauteville, 75010 Paris, France
+33 146 079 004
www.exyzt.org
contact@exyzt.org

Fair: Eme3 2005, Barcelona, Spain
Other cities: Possibly
Primary material: Scaffoldings
Photos: © Brice Pelleschi

The Extra Territorial Station (SET) was built in Poble Nou, an old industrial area of Barcelona, which is experiencing a high-speed renovation into a mixed area of companies and homes. SET is a structure of scaffolding installed on an empty site which was occupied by a house and a workspace for 30 people for ten years. The construction reaches a height of 52 feet, and its 23 tons of material took only four days to erect.

This ephemeral building had a toilet and showers in the court-yard; a kitchen equipped with ovens for making bread; a large reception and workroom on the first floor; and a projection room on the third floor. On the other levels tents were set up to accommodate participants, and the top floor was reserved as a viewing floor.

Exyzt is a group of architects who understand architecture as a form of activism and social investigation; they work in collaboration with other artists and graphic designers. These relations spawned the idea of covering the façade of the building in a sheet that received video projections.

SET was set up to house a show in which the participants were going to recreate the blast off of the Agbar tower (Jean Nouvel's building), which has become a symbol of both the neighborhood's and Barcelona's renovation. For one night SET was closed to the public and was used as a stage for a real-time video performance that ended in the Agbar tower becoming a rocket and flying away from Barcelona.

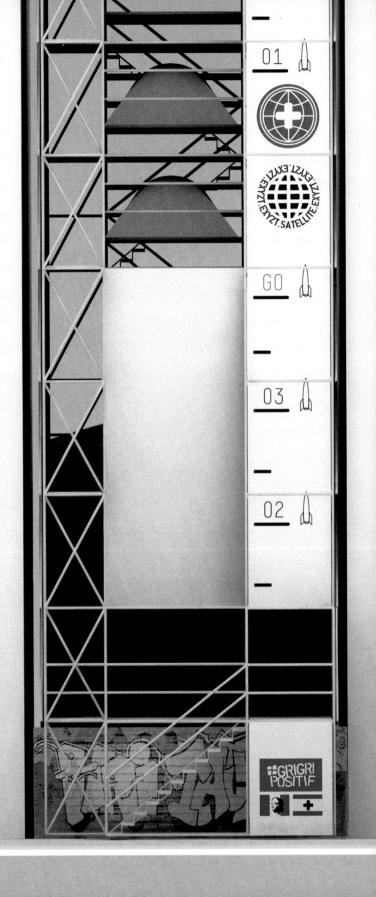

Photo collage

Photo collage

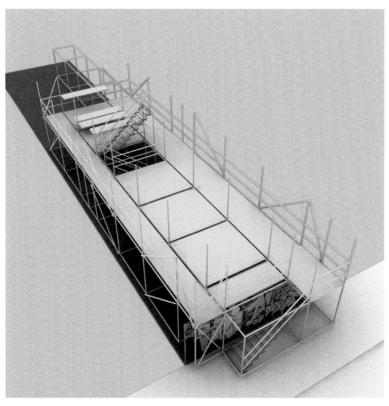

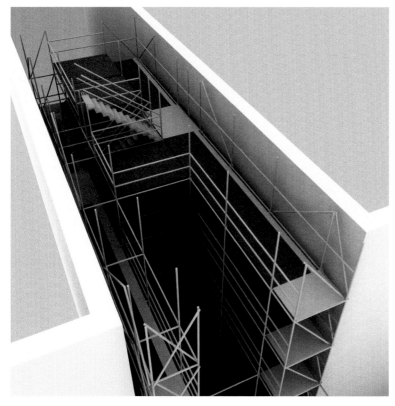

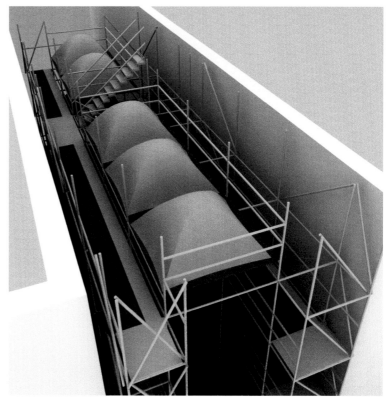

The structure made from scaffolding is a critical statement of conventional architecture, and presents different ways to construct and live in compact cities.

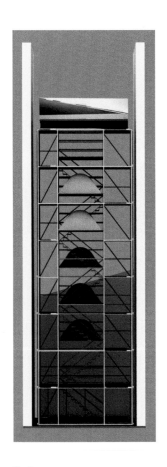

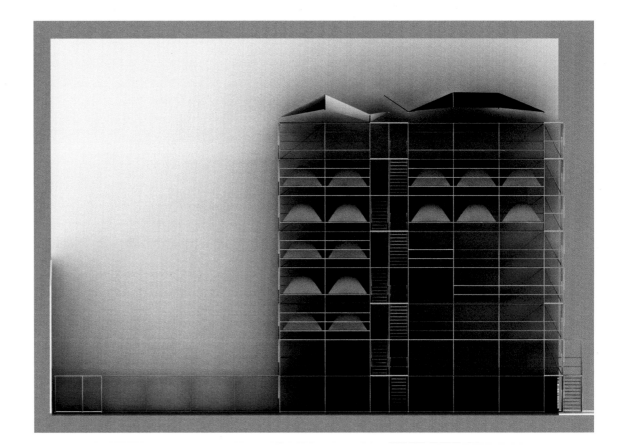

Sections

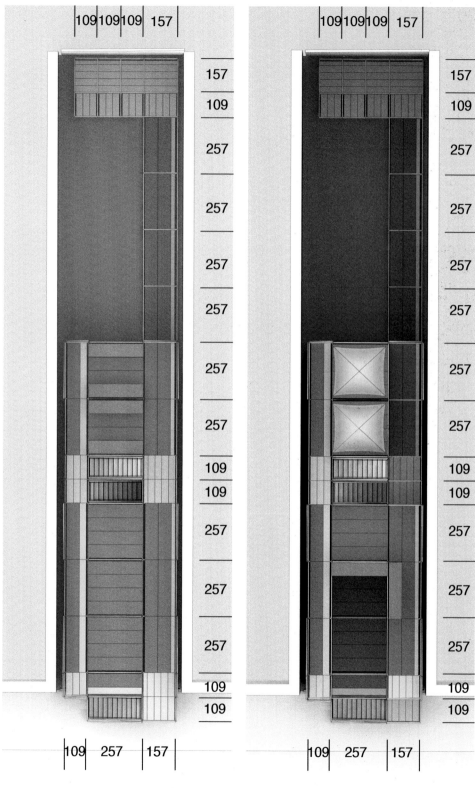

109	109	109	157	

157

109

257

257

257

257

257

257

109

109

257

257

257

109

109

109 | 257 | 157

Ground level

Part of the site was left open to create an interior courtyard, which separated the toilets from the rest of the construction and provided the building with the appropriate ventilation.

109	109	109	157	

157

109

257

257

257

257

257

257

109

109

257

257

257

109

109

109 | 257 | 157

Fourth level

Grohe

Architect: Klaus Schmidhuber

Address:
   Schmidhuber and Partner
   Nederlinger Strasse 21, 80638 Munich, Germany
         +49 89 157 997
www.schmidhuber.de
info@schmidhuber.de

Fair: ISH 2005, Frankfurt, Germany
Other cities: No
Primary material: Fluid lights
Photos: © Eberhard Franke

One of the problems that the designers of the Grohe stand had to overcome at the Frankfurt trade fair was to construct a pavilion with a plan of over 1200 square yards, in a hall whose height reached a maximum of thirteen feet, without making the mistake of creating an oppressive space.

However, the low height of the space eventually became the feature that unified the project. Eight large lamps of peculiar design were installed in the ceiling, which imitated both the fluid forms of the company's designs and the world of the sea. Although they were stuck close to the ceiling they gave the impression of floating, whereby the ceiling appeared higher, since the focus was drawn to the lights. The lights alternated between emanating green and blue light, which helped to create a pleasant and cozy atmosphere.

The furniture and the taps were lined up alternately facing the same direction as the lights to add harmony to the space. The back of the stand was reserved for the offices and the bar, which were installed in an independent volume, making them separate from the main space.

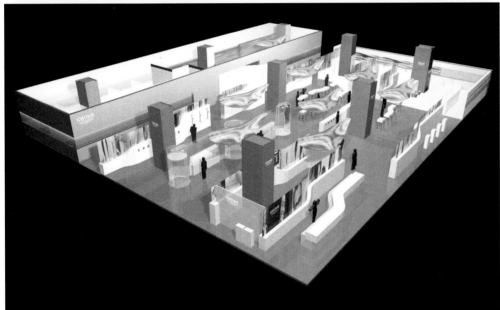

The changing colors of the lights softened the impact of the ceiling, which was very low in this part of the fair.

Perspective

The change of light intensity was meant to differentiate the bar from the rest of the pavilion. As such, the bar became a more relaxing zone of the fair.

Revitalisierung
Revitalisation

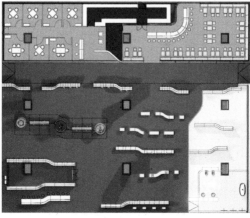

Plan

Atrio
Konzentration auf das Wesentliche
...k to the basics

Biopolis

Architect: Holzer Kobler

Address:
    Holzer Kobler
    Ankerstrasse 3, 8004 Zurich, Switzerland
        +41 1 240 52 00
www.holzerkobler.ch
mail@holzerkobler.ch

Fair: Expo 2002, Neuenburg, Switzerland
Other cities: No
Primary material: Light
Photos: © Holzer Kobler

The pharmaceutical company Novartis was in charge of organizing Biopolis, an exhibition aimed at showing the benefits of genetic engineering in the near future. The idea of the scene was to transport the visitors to the year 2022, where they could interact with the inhabitants of the future and visit the utopian city of Biopolis. A cycle of conferences took place alongside the exhibition, whose aim was to debate an issue that has caused controversy in some countries.

The exhibition focused on four large areas, and a specific space was created for each of them. As in other interactive museums, great care was taken in selecting the lighting, since in a space with so many screens and video projections it is necessary to guide the visitor and focus his or her attention on the videos. The entrance was a platform located at a high level, so the first vision of Biopolis was the large round table where images of different aspects of life were projected, and where visitors could take part in a multimedia program. This allowed visitors entering the exhibition to see others playing with the modules, which encouraged them to join in.

One of the most unusual videos was a series of interviews with eight inhabitants of Biopolis who spoke of the benefits of medicine, and of daily life in the future, where house-cleaning robots, intelligent fabric, and genetic engineering were commonplace.

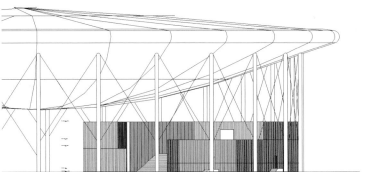

Elevation

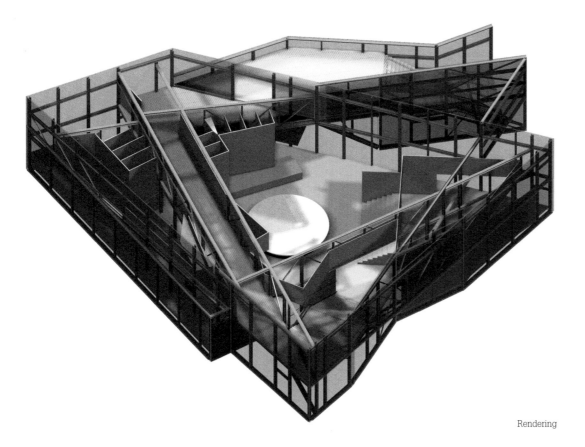

The irregularity of the structure was used to separate the different zones, and to create very different spaces for projecting the pavilion videos.

Rendering

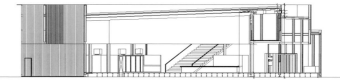

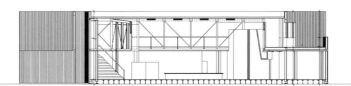

Sections

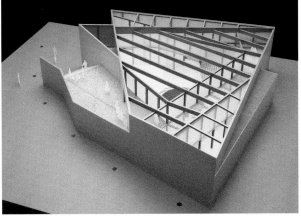

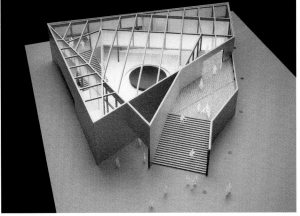

Scale model

The central space, with its large circular, interactive table, acted as a starting point for the rest of the interior. It also served as one of the stand's main attractions.

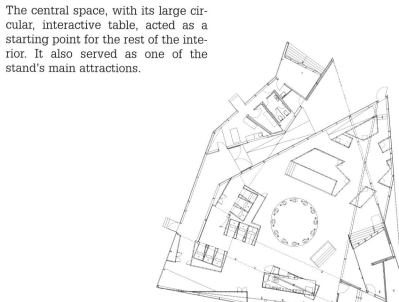

Basement floor

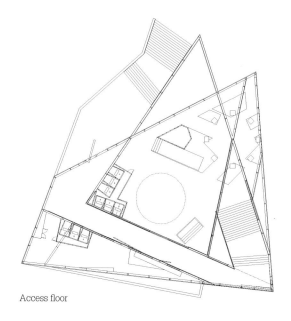

Access floor